Industry and Inequality

The achievement principle in work and
social status

Claus Offe
Translated by James Wickham

Edward Arnold

English translation and edition
© 1976 Edward Arnold (Publishers) Ltd

Authorized translation from the German
Leistungsprinzip und industrielle Arbeit
© 1970 Europaische Verlaganstalt

English edition first published 1976 by
Edward Arnold (Publishers) Ltd
25 Hill Street, London W1X 8LL

Cloth ISBN: 0 7131 5892 1
Paper ISBN: 0 7131 5893 X

Printed in Great Britain by Willmer Brothers Limited, Birkenhead

Industry and Inequality

For R K O
1943–1968

Contents

Translator's introduction   I

Author's introduction   I I

1 The theoretical framework   23

2 The concept of the achieving society   40

3 Occupational recruitment and occupational mobility within organizations: the functions of the achievement principle   47

4 The achievement principle and labour income   100

5 Conclusion: forms and consequences of the critique of the achievement principle   134

Abbreviations   145

References   147

Index   155

Translator's introduction

The recent resurgence of industrial militancy in the capitalist societies of the West has succeeded where conventional sociology has long failed—it has opened up to question the reason for the existence of wage and salary differentials and indeed of social inequality as a whole. Presumably it is fear of this new questioning that lies behind the claim in such countries as Britain that 'inflation is destroying the social fabric', for the social fabric is surely that delicately maintained state of affairs in which the way that income is distributed appears as inevitable, necessary and even just. Today, the different standards of living of, say, a coalminer and an industrial manager are beginning to appear as merely differences in power, and social inequality, such as differences in income, cannot for long merely rest on differences in power—inequality has to be justified and explained in such a way that the majority of the population (those who by definition are not privileged) accept it as morally right. Inequality has to be *legitimated*.

Claus Offe's study is it seems to me of major importance because it provides a sustained and critical analysis both of how this legitimation occurs and of how actual inequality arises. Certainly, orthodox sociology has long since 'rediscovered poverty' (the poor presumably knew about it all along, they just had the decency not to complain too loudly about it). However, such a 'rediscovery' has all too easily led to merely descriptive accounts of that poverty, focusing merely on a minority of 'the poor'. What sociology has not done is to ask seriously how our particular form of inequality comes to exist. It is to that question, tackled in relation to the organization of work in our society, that this book addresses itself.

In this introduction I wish to fulfil the normal task of a translator's introduction, helping the reader with difficulties that may arise from a text originally written in another language and deriving in part from traditions and debates he or she may not be familiar with. This is particularly necessary for those with little experience of academic sociology, for although this book can be seen as contributing to discussions within that discipline, I wish to argue that it is also of central political importance, particularly for anyone concerned with the development of the socialist movement in the

2 Industry and Inequality

'advanced' societies. After all, if socialism is about the creation of a society free of exploitation, then we need to understand how the inequality of contemporary society can appear to be so inevitable. The reader should therefore be warned that this introduction is also a commentary—unlike Offe's study itself, it is based on an explicit commitment both to socialist politics and to marxist science.

In modern industrial society, and especially in capitalist society, inequality, so Offe argues, is legitimated in terms of the 'achievement principle' (*Leistungsprinzip*). This can best be understood as that vague feeling that our individual work, achievement or performance (*Leistung*) will be rewarded, whether we consider this as the work we actually do or as what we have had to do in order to be able to carry out that work. The society claims to be 'fair' since 'achievement' provides a standard against which all the members of the society can be measured: the society is therefore an 'achieving society' (*Leistungsgesellschaft*).

Faced with such a claim, sociology has to go a lot further than just to point out the '*un*fairnesses' which do actually exist in these societies—the racial and religious discrimination, the class bias of the educational system etc. This sort of criticism may appear egalitarian, but in fact it accepts that fairness in terms of achievement is possible, that everyone *could* be stratified and rewarded according to their achievement. By contrast, a genuinely critical but nonetheless empirical sociology has to ask whether this form of fairness is even possible.

Whether in the factory or in the office, work is carried out within social institutions—'work organizations' (*Arbeitsorganisationen*). Clearly, it is individuals' income from work and their position within these work organizations which largely determine their position within society as a whole. Offe therefore sets himself the task of examining whether these organizations are of a form which allows their members' achievement to be the basis of their members' rewards. Such an analysis requires a re-examination of research from industrial and organizational sociology. Before this can be done however, the concepts used to approach this material have themselves to be clarified.

The first chapter of this study argues that work organizations can be classified in terms of the relationship between different tasks they involve—whether the organizations are 'task-continuous status organizations' (*Aufgabekontinuerliche-Status-Organisationen*) or 'task-discontinuous status organizations' (*Aufgabe-diskontinuerliche-Status-Organisationen*). In the former type, to be higher in the organization's status hierarchy is to have more of the same skills than someone in a lower position, while in the latter type someone in a lower position has *different* skills. When this is the case, Offe argues that control in the organization cannot occur through the technical requirements of the task, since the 'superior' person is in fact unable to judge whether these are being fulfilled. Instead, control must occur through the 'peripheral' elements of the work role—those normative and ideological requirements which are defined as necessary for the task but which are not related to its technical fulfilment. Organizational and technological changes in the nature of work are, Offe claims, making this second form of control increasingly predominant.

Since the achievement principle as an all-embracing ideology is not of course neatly written down, the second chapter examines it as a model of society, asking what is necessary for the principle to be the sole basis of individuals' rewards from work. It emerges that if, in the society as a whole, all individuals are going to be placed 'fairly' in a hierarchy according to their achievement, then the work organizations of that society will have to fulfil two conditions. Firstly, they will have to possess a unified and objectifiable scale of achievement (*Leistungsskala*): everyone must be able to know and agree how everyone is ranked. Secondly, there must be competent authorities who are able to assess individuals in terms of this scale; superiors must be able to apply this scale.

The empirical chapters of the study use the classifications of the first chapter to demonstrate that, at least in the work organizations of contemporary capitalist society, these two conditions are not fulfilled. The achievement principle is not and cannot be applied: studies from an organizational and industrial sociology are analysed to show that neither recruitment and promotion (chapter 3) nor income (chapter 4) do depend upon performance or achievement, however defined. Furthermore, organizational and technological changes have made it impossible for this to ever be the case.

However, the achievement principle is not just an ideology, it is also built into the work organizations of industrial society: recruitment and promotion procedures are carried out as if they were in terms of achievement. In this situation these procedures have become increasingly organized in terms of symbolic substitutes for performance, so that what they reward is not technical performance, but rather the demonstrated acceptance by the individual of the organization's power relationships. Similarly, differential income from work is revealed as depending purely upon a consensus in society that some jobs deserve greater rewards than others. Attempts to fix wage levels (and in particular wage differentials) 'fairly' in terms of job evaluation or time-and-motion study are thus this normative consensus dressed up in pseudoscientific garb. It follows then that the achievement principle does not even any longer fulfil its original and liberative role, namely ensuring that everyone should be judged according to their contribution to the development of the productive forces of society (and hence to the welfare of the society's members). The insistence that rewards should be distributed *differentially* to *individuals* does not mean that the principle itself is fulfilled, merely that people are constrained to act *as if it were*. As a result the existing distribution of power is cemented and the development of the productive forces hindered. The existing form of inequality is therefore revealed as not just repressive but also irrational.

Offe's argument is located within two traditions of social thought which are at first sight completely opposed: recent German marxism and American functionalist sociology. Since much of the difficulty of the study derives from the way in which it uses these two traditions, it is worth examining them in more detail.

From the marxism of the 'Frankfurt school', Offe derives a concern with the critical analysis of ideology—of the way in which the dominant thought of a society can be explained by the basic reality of that society which the thought operates to disguise. Critical theory, as this school of marxism has come to be known, opposes the rationality of its thought to the irrationality of contemporary capitalist society and to the irrationality of the thought which accepts that society.

Above all, therefore, critical theory offers a basic critique of the 'social sciences'. Academic disciplines, such as 'positive' economics, 'behavioural' psychology and 'scientific' sociology may claim to analyse the society within which they exist, but in fact they can only mystify it. Instead of contributing to genuine understanding, these disciplines offer only confusion which renders more solid the exploitation and irrationality of contemporary capitalism. This occurs not despite, but precisely because of, their alleged neutrality. The rhetoric of 'measurement' and 'variables' is all predicated on the assumption that human society can be analysed in terms of facts and laws. This ignores the historical nature of society, such that capitalism is qualitatively different to the social forms which preceded it and has itself only a limited historical existence. Further, 'positivist' social science is blind to the fact that any study of society is itself located within society, and so necessarily is both affected by and affects that society. To the extent that the social sciences refuse to tackle these problems, they justify the existing society by making it appear 'natural' and eternal: they deny the possibility of alternative forms of social production and organization. By contrast, critical theory is 'critical' because its analysis is explicitly based both on the historical limitation of contemporary society and on a commitment to changing it.

In the marxist tradition, and essentially unlike all more strictly sociological thought, the basis of society, the forces of production are understood as consisting of relationships both between people *and* between people and nature. It is in this sense that marxism is a 'materialism'. Since this study is concerned to analyse the internal structure of *work* organizations, it is important to consider this argument in more detail.

For marxism, work in capitalist society is understood as essentially collective action, involving social relationships of both cooperation and exploitation. Thus, so long as the society remains a capitalist one, the capitalist (or better, the representatives of capital) are as necessary for the work task to be achieved as are the workers themselves. For example, in his analysis of the labour process in *Capital*,[1] Marx discusses the necessary role of the capitalist in bringing workers together in a group and uniting them with the machinery and raw materials needed for their tasks; in *The origins of the State and private property*, Engels argues that the division of labour and the accompanying development of the productive ability of society has been the reverse side of the increase in exploitation throughout history.[2] In capitalism, however, both tendencies reach a peak. While cooperation develops to a greater extent than ever before, in that actual production becomes an almost entirely collective process, this also creates the basis for the removal of exploitation—for the creation of a society where the work of all can be for the benefit of all.

However, until that should happen, although the wealth of society is socially produced, what is produced and how it is distributed is not decided by any collective public and democratic decision, but rather by private decisions in line with the dictates of profit and of the market—dictates which necessarily benefit only a minority. The 'relations of production' are the social relationships between people through which this occurs—the institution of private property itself. It is important to see that both 'forces of production' and 'relations of production' are sets of social relationships between largely the same people: they are neither things (machinery etc.) nor different groups of people.

Marx of course goes further than merely pointing this out. He states first that the private (and hence irrational) character of economic decisions begins to hamper the full development of those

[1] K. Marx, *Capital* I, ch. 7, 'The labour process and the process of producing surplus value' (1867; quoted from Everyman edition, New York 1974).
[2] F. Engels, *The origin of the family, the state and private property* (1875; quoted from the 1972 reprint, London). Engels particularly stresses the parallel development of exploitation and productive ability in the case of the first example of the division of labour—that between the sexes.

potentialities of society which collective labour itself has brought about; secondly, that this tension will ultimately lead to social conflict in the form of the class struggle which will align the form of production with the form of distribution by collectivizing them both. In marxist discussion then, terms such as the contradiction between collective production and private appropriation, between use value and exchange value, between the forces of production and the relations of production, all designate aspects of this basic public-private opposition which capitalism has created and which will be ultimately transcended by the transformation of the system itself.

The idea of a 'lack of fit' between different aspects of a society is also present in the other major theoretical influence on the present study, structural functionalist theory. Here the social order of society is seen as maintained by an interlocking set of shared 'norms' (agreed rules for action) accepted by the members of society, while the different institutions in the society are all seen as being related by the way they contribute to society as a whole—by their 'functions'. Especially in the works of Talcott Parsons,[3] society is therefore seen as an integrated 'social system', and this term points out the essential similarity between structural functionalist theory and marxism. Unlike much recent sociology, for example the schools of thought going under the labels of symbolic interactionism and ethnomethodology, both marxism and functionalism are concerned to explain individuals and institutions in terms of their interrelationships within society as a whole. This is a similarity which the political connotations of the two has tended to disguise, and at a theoretical level Offe's work is important because his approach utilizes this shared concern.

However, if this is to be done, structural functionalism has to be detached from its conservative political commitment. Critical theory enables us to see that what functionalism terms norms are not the emanation of some basic social harmony, but essentially ideology—in C. Wright Mills's phrase, 'master symbols of legitimation'. Equally, while functionalist theory allows that some parts of the social system may not 'fit' with others, it sees this as a question of 'strain', as a problem which will necessarily cause the development of further social mechanisms to contain and control the initial tension. The marxist argument, by contrast, sees this 'strain' as a contradiction which can lead to the transformation of the system itself.

[3] Talcott Parsons, *The social system* (London 1970). Parsons's work is renowned for its difficulty and abstruse terminology, and this has tended to obscure the extent of his theoretical contributions. A simple introduction to his arguments is provided by Edward C. Devereux, 'Parson's sociological theory' in M. Black (ed.), *The social theories of Talcott Parsons* (Englewood Cliffs, NJ, 1961).

Another major influence of functionalist theory is the insistence that a social institution like a firm, just as society itself, must be conceptualized as a system of roles, not as a group of people. It is the fact that people are in roles that makes it possible for them to exist as a group, indeed, to exist at all. Roles are defined by norms, which describe the rights and duties of their occupants and which crucially prescribe how the individual is to be recruited into the role in the first place. Functionalist theory sees the trend of history as being towards an ever greater 'universality'—the increasing application of the same social rules to all individuals. In particular, it is claimed that roles are increasingly filled purely on the basis of merit. In other words, workers' promotion and recruitment depend not on their family connections, their race, religion or sex but purely on how well they carry out their tasks. It is here, in the formulation of social change as being from *ascription* to *achievement*, that functionalist theory and the ideology of capitalist society become almost interchangeable.

For critical theory, such a remarkable convergence between ideology and alleged explanation is hardly surprising, but this does not mean to say that functionalist theory can be simply dismissed. Indeed, functionalist theory provides the basis for the development of the concepts of 'system problem' and 'system contradiction' which have been at the centre of the more recent work of Offe and of Jürgen Habermas.[4] The concept of 'system contradiction' is also crucial to this study.

As writers such as Lockwood and Mouzelis have pointed out, we have to distinguish rigorously between *contradiction* and *conflict*.[5] The class struggle, for example, is an obvious example of social *conflict*: it is a clash between two opposing groups of people. As we have seen, however, Marx argues that it is itself produced by the clash between the forces of production and the relations of production, and that these are actually sets of social relations involving largely the same groups of people. Marx is arguing that these social relationships, the collective production of wealth and its private appropriation, are in the long run incompatible—that they are in *contradiction*.

Marx's own scientific work was of course mainly concerned with the economic aspect of this contradiction, which has unfortunately led to marxism being seen as largely an economic theory. Such an

[4] Claus Offe, *Strukturprobleme des kapitalistischen Staates* (Frankfurt a.M. 1972); Jurgen Habermas, *Legitimations-probleme im Spätkapitalismus* (Frankfurt a.M. 1974). Offe's recent work is critically discussed in *Working Papers on the Kapitalistate* 2 (1973), 60–69.
[5] D. Lockwood, 'Social integration and system integration', in G. K. Zollschran and W. Hirsh (eds.), *Explorations in social change* (London 1964), 244–56; N. Mouzelis, 'Social integration and system integration: some reflections on a fundamental distinction', *BJS* 25 (4) (1974), 395–409.

interpretation ignores that capitalist *economic* crisis can always be resolved in a capitalist fashion: an economic crisis by no means provokes the automatic transformation of capitalism, but can instead lead to the development of new forms of economic and social integration. These do not resolve the economic contradiction, they merely displace it, so that it manifests itself in a different form. This is exactly analagous to Offe's argument: in the absence of the social transformation of the 'achieving society', the impossibility of distributing rewards in terms of achievement leads to them being distributed in terms of the 'peripheral' elements of the work role. While this apparently solidifies the existing form of inequality, it also blocks the development of the productive forces of society and ultimately exacerbates the contradiction still further.

The difference between contradiction and conflict means therefore that we cannot make any automatic assumptions as to how such a social contradiction will be manifested in social conflict, let alone as to the outcome of that conflict. Marx himself can be criticized for making precisely such an assumption. Indeed Offe in his more recent work has explicitly rejected the idea that the manual working class is automatically the 'carrier' of the basic contradiction of capitalist society—it is not necessarily the social group which will form the basis of a movement for a new society. Analysis of capitalism must begin with its contradictions, and not with its conflicts.

This refusal to *begin* the analysis of capitalism with a focus on classes is similar to the approach of recent 'structuralist' marxists influenced by Louis Althusser. In particular, the latter have pointed out that to start with a class analysis means to treat classes as the 'building blocks' of society, taking them as essentially given, and thus being unable to explain how the classes are created in the first place. All this quite apart from the well known problems of defining who is 'really' in the ruling class and who is 'really' in the working class (where do managers and whitecollar workers belong?). Instead, we have to understand capitalism as a mode of production—as a way of organizing the production and appropriation of wealth—and only after this move to the analysis of the classes this mode *creates.*[6]

Thus both Offe and 'structuralist' marxists reject a narrowly economic and a narrowly sociological interpretation of marxism. However, while the latter have gone on to attempt to develop a theory of politics, and hence of the class struggle itself, Offe has here taken a different path. This study is merely concerned to work out the consequences of the contradiction between an ideology

[6] This is brought out very clearly in the controversy between Nicos Poulantzas and Ralph Milliband over the nature of the modern capitalist state and how it is to be analysed: see their articles in R. Blackburn (ed.), *Ideology and social science* (London 1972).

which claims that individuals are rewarded in terms of their achievement and productive organization which make it more and more impossible for this actually to happen. However, once we accept that capitalism is not initially about classes, then clearly if we wish to understand the chances of transforming it into socialism, it is with its contradictions that the analysis must begin.

Until the mid 1960s political commentators frequently proclaimed 'the end of ideology'—that capitalism had overcome its contradictions and would expand for ever into a smooth future of increasing consumer affluence and political quiescence. For such ideologues, marxism was as out of date as cloth caps and the working class itself. The changed political situation today makes such statements themselves seem like voices from an already almost forgotten past.

Offe's study is itself in many ways a product of the 'end of ideology' thesis. Like it, he essentially accepts that Keynesian economics have enabled governments to 'manage' the economy so that at least old-style economic crises are behind us. Once again, possibly a dubious assumption today.

Nonetheless, and however paradoxical it sounds, it is the acceptance of this assumption which is the motive force for Offe's own inquiry—for if we accept that capitalism is basically contradictory, then the containment of its contradictions (such as economic crisis itself) can only be at the cost of producing further contradictions. However, the general argument is clearly not invalidated by the implicit assumption that economic crises are things of the past: of itself, economic crisis can only accelerate the changes in work organizations which are analysed here.

I have already commented that the study is marked by a silence or at least a scepticism as to the political potential of the traditionally-defined working class. This is a position doubtless fuelled by the political impotence of the class in many Western societies, notably in the most 'advanced' ones of the USA and West Germany from which most of Offe's evidence is drawn. However, Offe also appears to accept what the 'end of ideology' thesis also stressed, namely the end of the manual working class as a clearly and 'obviously' defined cultural entity. If in lifestyle and 'culture' manual workers are integrated into the society, what possibility does this class provide for an alternative society? It is interesting to note that Offe's own analysis provides a possible explanation for precisely this integration: namely, that if control in work organizations is through 'technical rules', it is hardly a problem should the worker possess a distinct cultural identity. However, once control is through the worker's 'normative orientations', the necessary control in work will depend precisely upon the removal of any basic cultural differences between him and his superiors. Offe's analysis therefore implies that modern work conditions require a much greater cultural similarity between all levels of the work force than was ever the case in the more traditional industries.

This argument suggests a paradox: the removal of cultural opposition within capitalist society occurs precisely when the possibility of a total transformation of that society has never been greater. The work organizations of capitalism have only recently developed to the extent that the inequality which they produce is in fact now unnecessary, yet this very development removes precisely that cultural 'space within' which was the traditional locus of socialist movements.

Such an extremely practical paradox can only be resolved by a politics which goes beyond the mere reaction to the effects of economic crisis. Offe's analysis reveals as mere ideology the assumption that the only reliable basis for economic life—for the production of wealth needed by all the members of society—is an appeal to the individual's self-interest. An egalitarian society—one where differences in individual status were subject to democratic and public control, where production was determined in a genuinely public discussion, and where the division of labour was dramatically curtailed—is now no longer utopian. Instead, it is the achieving society itself, that society of desperate striving individuals and continued calls for higher productivity, which is revealed as historically superseded.

At a time when workers are being told that the mere defence of their living standards will destroy the fabric of society, it is imperative to realize how redundant that particular fabric is. And this realization cannot be just an intellectual one, it must become part of the working-class movement itself. Mere defence of sectional or class interests cannot of itself produce such a realization, indeed it is doomed to defeat without the *rational* conviction that an alternative to the present is not merely desirable, but is a real historical possibility. It is to be hoped that this study can help to reveal that possibility and in some small way contribute to its realization.

James Wickham

Dublin, July 1975

Author's introduction

In contemporary capitalist industrial societies, the system of official self-imagery and self-explanation is dominated by the concept of the achieving society. Yet, surprisingly enough, sociology has rarely taken the concept seriously or subjected it to critical and empirical investigation. Within German social science, the few exceptions to this rule include one essay by Ralf Dahrendorf[1] and a study by Oskar Negt entitled 'Anticipating the authoritarian achieving society'.[2] Here Negt analyses the image of society held by the industrial and military elites, and goes on to deduce from this the likely trends in the development of society as a whole.

Negt argues that, since the elite groups hold power as well as an image of society, the image itself can be realized in political decisions which in turn shape the structure of society. This image of society is two-sided. Positively, it prescribes: it presents the picture of a highly efficient achieving society, a society in which the rights and privileges of every social group depend strictly on what is held to be that group's contribution to the total social product. Negatively, it proscribes: it denies alternatives in theory and provides the legitimation for suppressing them in practice. Categories and institutions are suppressed which could form the basis of a democratic public opinion, or indeed of any explicitly political opinion, as are categories and institutions which would enable people in any way to determine their own needs through open discussion. In Negt's words: 'The basic categories of the liberal self-understanding, concepts such as interest, compromise, conflict and public discussion lose in reality their constitutive importance for late capitalist society.'[3]

In the course of this process of erosion of the genuinely public realm, all that is left over is the fiction of an abstract common interest. While certainly this common interest fits neatly into what the military-industrial elites define as prosperity, it can in no way be presented as the expression of a conscious common need. It is

[1] R. Dahrendorf, 'Industrielle Fertigkeiten und soziale Schichtung', *KZfSS* 8 (1956), 540–68.
[2] O. Negt, 'In Erwartung der autoritären Leistungsgesellschaft', in G. Schäfer and C. Nedelmann (eds.), *Der CDU-Staat* (Munich 1967), 200–237.
[3] *Ibid.*, 204.

B

significant that this 'common welfare' is in fact defined negatively rather than positively: welfare is merely the absence of mass poverty.

The notion of an achieving society thus provides a convenient imagery: in fact the historical function of the concept was simply to legitimate privilege. Today this aspect is still taken up with great gusto by the official authorities. For example, an annual report of the German Industrialists' Association can state: 'If we describe our society as in industrial society, then the entrepreneur is a key figure. For its further development our society relies upon the entrepreneur, that social role which represents the importance of individual initiative.'[4] This sort of justification is trotted out with an obstinacy and a rigidity that are in themselves suspicious. One begins to suspect that we are dealing here with a defensive ritual against obsolescence, against the realization that the much-touted functional connection between entrepreneurial initiative, overall social productivity and the legitimated privileges of certain clearly defined social groups has now dissolved. From the shadowy realm of the early capitalist 'creative entrepreneur', individuals are cited as witnesses to that ethos which used to link risk-taking, initiative and the will to innovate for social change. Today, however, the functions of socioeconomic dynamism which these entrepreneurs allegedly filled are now largely carried out by the technostructure of the large-scale bureaucratic organization and its decision-making processes. For this reason alone, while the ideology of the achieving society may be frequently cited, it cannot any longer be explained merely in terms of its one function of maintaining the will to individualistic effort at the level necessary for society to continue.

In this situation the other side of the ideology becomes prominent, namely its depoliticizing and restrictive components. The ideas which are linked to a model of society organized exclusively on criteria of efficiency now take on the character of a defensively constructed myth—a myth which strengthens the bulwarks of the social structure against alternative models of social production and distribution. The ideology of the achieving society entails rules of social and political action, and their results amount to a structure of repression which can be extrapolated into the future, blocking the articulation, let alone the satisfaction, of social interests and social needs. The social imagery of the achieving society is dominated by the abstract notion of 'efficiency'. This implies not only the repression of those *practical* desires which cannot demonstrate any functional contribution to the overall system of achievement, but also discrimination against any attempt to challenge the criteria of achievement and efficiency through the framework of concepts of use value. The trends in the development of late capitalist societies

---

[4] *Jahresbericht des BDI* (Annual Report of the Association of German Industrialists) 1966, 34.

towards technocracy and authoritarianism have often been described —given such trends, the importance is obvious of the fact that the authorities themselves continually refer to the model of an achieving society.

As a way of conceptualizing the organization of the whole society, this ideology thus fulfils two functions. First, it legitimates social status; secondly, it represses social alternatives. It would appear now that, of these two functions, the second is becoming the more important.

If one investigates the *conceptual structure* of this whole complex of ideas, then a remarkable emasculation of its descriptive and normative components emerges. The ideas refer at the same time both to the current *characteristics* and to the immanent *programme of development* of the politicoeconomic system of late capitalist societies. In other words, the ideas simultaneously provide an interpretation of the present and offer, through this interpretation, the future as the extrapolation of an existing trend.

Since it does this, the complex of ideas satisfies one of the general criteria of ideology. Ideologies are defined in that, firstly, they *consolidate* an existing social condition with justifications derived from the status quo, and, secondly, they shield and *guard* the existing society against its own historical alternatives, denying the historicity, the historical limitedness, of any given social condition. In so far as they do this, ideologies ensure the good conscience and analytical poverty of the historical consciousness that they express. At this point there appears a second characteristic of ideology. Interpretive schemas become ideologies (i.e. both *false* and *ruling* consciousness) when, in the fulfilment of their double function of consolidation and defence, they fall into irresolvable contradictions. On the one hand, an ideology can actually manage to create a voluntary consensus as to the definition of the just society, thereby completely fulfilling its legitimating function. Yet, in the moment that it does this, it must fail in its other function of theoretically and practically nullifying the dynamic of history. The achievement of a complete and voluntary consensus means the release of the utopian elements of the ideology: instead of stopping the movement of history, the ideology becomes its driving force. On the other hand, an ideology can erect effective defences against the historical alternatives. Yet if these are completely successful and any notion of a possible social world apart from the existing one is thereby obliterated, the present can only be legitimated by reference to itself, thus increasing the system problems of integrating and legitimating a structure of domination and privilege which is in fact historically created.

These two alternatives entail nothing less than the conceptual contradictoriness of ideologies: the complete achievement of their consensus-forming function is incompatible with the achievement of their repressive function, and vice versa.

In this sense, then, the formula of an 'achieving society' is revealed as an ideology. In practical political action, its results have the function of silencing any social group articulating needs and interests that transcend the existing system. This defensive character of the achieving society is manifested in its authoritarian implications: wherever there are social groups which claim their privileges and their dominant positions on the grounds that these are *functional*, then the action and development of these groups becomes shaped by the defence against competing power groups, a defence which can go as far as the destruction of the conditions under which these opponents can develop. Certainly this has costs: the prescribed interpretation of the 'achieving society' is eventually maintained only defensively, becoming less and less plausible, increasingly inadequate in its categories and wielding a diminished power of legitimation. In the following section I would like to list the three points on which the thesis can be based that the 'achieving society' is self-contradictory as a framework for understanding society as a whole.

1   In capitalist social systems, the functional groups of capital owners and the leading personnel of bureaucratic organizations are clearly privileged: they have chances of influence and claims on social expenditure which are denied to other groups. Yet, *as groups*, both of them face a loss of function, so that it is impossible for the privileges specific to them as groups to be interpreted and legitimated as the necessary rewards for that achievement ethic which originally determined the level of total social productivity. Under the conditions of an advanced and organized capitalism, only with difficulty can management be considered as the collective subject of the economic initiative functions which shape the total social structure (and the same applies to any form of leadership group which claims recognition of its privileges as being functionally necessary as incentives or rewards). Both political and economic power have been subjected to a process of monopolization which has concentrated initiative functions in less identifiable decision-making centres, in the large socially-organized interest groups and in the state apparatus, which itself has continually expanded the parameters of its intervention. As a result the unity of the owners of capital as a functional social group is becoming a fiction. If there are initiative functions which can be considered important enough for a claim to privilege to be based on them, then they are those functions fulfilled by the bureaucracies of the individual branches of that state apparatus, the large voluntary associations and the political parties as well as the large, market-dominating corporations.

Yet within these structures there is no single group of people which can be clearly delimited, so that there is no group which could legitimate its privileges in the way in which the achieving society model prescribes, namely through decisionmaking functions which can be ascribed to individuals. At the level of the overall society there is an ever clearer tendency towards the concentration of decision-making functions within a few identifiable power centres. However, *inside* these large-scale organizations there is a counter-vailing process apparent towards the diffusion of the decision-making subjects. The decision-making processes themselves are becoming subordinated to a division of labour; both differing functional groups of specialists and differing levels of the authority hierarchy parti-cipate in the decision-making process, so that it cannot any longer be interpreted as merely the way in which a 'leadership' expresses its will. Galbraith has recently pointed out this component of the notion of 'organized capitalism': 'It is not to individuals but to organizations that power in the business enterprise and power in society has passed. Modern economic society can only be understood as an effort, wholly successful, to synthesize by organization a group personality far superior for its purposes to a natural person.'[5]

According to Galbraith, then, decisions can no longer be ascribed to individuals, but have to be ascribed to organized systems, which themselves are made up of members of groups which differ both in status and in qualifications. Within these organizations decisions and strategies are produced by the synthesis of information and of differing particular interests, and, given the structure of the organization, this occurs in a way which cannot be influenced by specific individuals or even by clearly delimitable groups. As in the production sphere in general, but in particular and most strikingly at the level of 'management' decision-making, a process is emerging which could be called the 'factual societization of action systems'. It follows that the attempt to ascribe structural changes in society to the will of individually acting subjects, or even to definable functional groups, clearly amounts to a strategic fiction. The legiti-mating model of the achieving society exhausts itself as the claimed congruence of economically privileged groups and structure-shaping initiative functions becomes both socially invisible and analytically disprovable.

2   The boundaries of those functional groups whose decisions do in fact ensure economic efficiency increasingly diverge from the boundaries of the economically privileged groups. The very concept of 'functional group' is losing its relevance for identifying the decision-making actors in the economy. Nonetheless, the economically privileged themselves hang on to the myth of the achieving society: for them at least privilege and function still go together. This is one side of the argument: the other becomes apparent when one

[5] J. K. Galbraith, *The new industrial state* (London 1960), 60.

investigates the actual situation of the economic system and its overall dynamic. It becomes questionable whether these can be explained from the actions of social actors (whether conceived of as individuals or as groups) and plausible that the present prosperity and expansion is basically ensured by the politically organized controls and regulatory mechanisms incorporated in a Keynesian-inspired policy of boom and full employment.

In all Western capitalist societies, once they have developed beyond a certain level, the state has taken over the legal or at least the factual responsibility for maintaining a high level of economic prosperity. This responsibility is manifested in the separate planning imperatives of full employment, price stability, balance of payments equilibrium and economic growth. The state activities have expanded to an extent that makes rather questionable the common form of speech which describes the state as maintaining the *framework* of the economy—such a description may minimize the phenomenon and so distract from its real nature. 'The responsibility (for assuring economic stability at near full employment) of the federal government is widely accepted, but the policies are still thought of as providing a favourable environment for private enterprise. In a sense they do, but . . . would it not be more descriptive and perceptive—and honest—to speak of these policies and actions as guaranteeing the national income?'[6]

The answer this question implies leads to the assumption that those initiative functions upon which the creation and continual re-creation of equilibrium conditions depend have in fact now been transferred into the sphere of action of the state apparatus, where they are carried out by the executive branches of the state. The analytical value of such an assumption is not reduced by the proviso that the state's new function of guaranteeing prosperity can only be carried out with the help of non-state-organized decision-making centres and, above all, under the restrictive conditions which these set. The other obvious reservation which also has to be made does not challenge the validity of the basic assumption either. Of course, it is quite true that only according to the ideology is the *form* of the political organization of these economic initiative functions so structured that there are *democratically* distributed chances of participating in the decision-making process, such that its actual *results* can be controlled. However, even if this were the case, it is still likely that there would be a problem of legitimacy: as the state power acquires more functions it also requires an increased legitimation. As more processes are transferred from a 'state-free' sector into that of public administration, so the circle grows of

[6] M. Lovenstein, 'Guaranteed income and traditional economics', in R. Theobald (ed.), *The guaranteed income* (New York 1966); cf. also R. Heilbronner, *The limits of American capitalism* (New York 1966).

groups which can influence the execution of administrative strategies, either because they can impede them by applying a veto or because they can further them by providing legitimacy or obedience. Thus, in the case in which economic functions are transferred to the political authorities, the thesis outlined in the previous section is confirmed : in both cases the monopolization of decision-making power and the diffusion of decision-making actors occur together and are causally interconnected.

At this macroeconomic level, then, structural changes are destroying in two ways the basis for an interpretation of the social mechanisms of distribution in terms of an achievement society model. First, the allocation of resources to specific groups occurs less and less in line with what would be expected by interpretive schema which sees reimbursements as rewards for, and incentives to, achievement. To the extent that organized, anonymous and monopolistic decision-making centres take over from elite groups those functions which can be visibly exercised by groups or individuals, it becomes more and more difficult to legitimate the privileges distributed to different groups in terms of being 'rewards'. When the question is posed of what contribution a particular group has made in order to be able to claim such reimbursements as 'rewards', there can only be an empty answer: the question has to be warded off with myth-building. Secondly, the same position is reached in the case of the other asserted connection between achievement and remuneration upon which a legitimation of privilege could rest—it could be claimed that remuneration has the character of a necessary incentive, which must be provided if the whole reproduction* process is not to come to a standstill. However, the factual politicization of society (the growth in the influence of state power in the reproduction process) has reduced material incentives as a control mechanism to, at most, partial functions within a system of authoritarian total administration. Precisely those adaptation problems of capitalist industrial societies which incentives are claimed to solve seem in fact to be soluble through administrative rather than market-oriented controls. Investment possibilities are created and regulated through political decisions, and it is these that produce the level of economic activity necessary to ensure continued social reproduction, a level of economic activity which could not be created by the incentives resulting merely from profit-oriented capital accumulation.

3   Finally, the categorical relevance of the concept of the achieving society is becoming questionable, as is therefore its legiti-

---

* Marxist theory stresses that it is necessary to analyse not only the conditions under which actual production occurs within any society, but also the conditions for the society as a whole to continue as an ongoing process —the process of social reproduction. (*Trans.*)

mating validity. The achieving society concept postulates an equivalence between the contribution and the remuneration of specific
groups, yet this is being violated by those very developments which
are intended to maintain the existing social structure. This applies
above all to the growing amount of transfer payments and subsidies to those economic actors who either are, temporarily or
permanently, outside the sphere of the labour market or who would,
without such subsidies, be pushed out of the capital market. 'A
large number of people are unable to earn their living because they
are too old, too young, too mentally or physically ill. . . . Transfer
payments indicate a vital growing area, where "work" and "pay"
are not closely related.'[7] The contradiction between such institutionalized claims on income and the principles of the achieving
society can be softened through two varieties of post facto rationalizations. Transfer payments can be interpreted as being merely
temporary and thus as *exceptional solutions* which cancel themselves out over time; alternatively they can be fixed according to
criteria of achievement ability—i.e. transfer payments can be fixed
in line with the income which the recipient intends to gain or is
expected to gain in the labour market. Conservative social welfare
policy planned on these lines may have been practical when it was
dealing with problems caused by the *failure* of the traditional welfare
systems such as the extended family; it is no longer practical when,
as is now the case, the problems which for their solution require
an ever-increasing extension of non-performance-based transfer
payments are themselves being produced by the *immanent* developmental trends of the labour markets of industrial societies.

At this stage it will be enough merely to give some examples of
these trends. It is functionally necessary that training periods are
extended, or, to put it another way, that individuals spend less time
in a labour situation determined by the market and therefore in
a situation which would enable the fiction of a remuneration based
on performance to be maintained. Whichever way this is seen, the
market relationship is temporarily loosened. The same loosening
of the link to the market and the same impossibility of equating
contribution and remuneration applies at the end of working life.
In the present situation, with its trends towards institutionalized
inflation combined with a long-term lowering of the pension age
and rising life-expectancy, this period of life can only be coped
with by an income which is collectively and politically determined.
Finally, the necessity of disengaging work or achievement status
from the income-level status of social groups results from the effects
of industrial innovation on the *employment level* and on the
employment structure. Labour has to be made redundant for either
structural or cyclical reasons, and this produces an increased

[7] Theobald, *The guaranteed income*, 87, 113.

number of people to whom, if only because their political loyalty has to be ensured, living standards have to be granted which do not depend on the market. This, together with the general imperatives of economic policy, is responsible for those tendencies towards an increasing secondary income distribution which overlays both the results of the primary income distribution and the group-specific differences which the latter creates.

The combined effect of this type of phenomena seems to be the creation of a situation where growing sections of the population lose their relationship to the concrete processes of market-valued production, with the result that their share of the total social product can no longer be determined by market criteria. What all these phenomena have in common is that they cannot be explained in terms of a model of cultural lag, in terms of, for example, the 'backwardness' of agrarian or family structures. Rather they are being continually created and re-created by the basic conditions under which advanced capitalist societies reproduce themselves.

It is even becoming plausible to hypothesize that the concept of full employment itself is becoming ambiguous and contradictory. The Keynesian tradition still sees full employment of *capital* and full employment of *labour* as compatible aims which can be achieved together through the same economic policy. However, under contemporary conditions in which the overall dynamism of the economy is dependent on technical innovations which are both capital and education intensive, this assumption is becoming dubious. It becomes questionable whether the absorption of all the capital available for investment will still lead to the full employment of the total social labour power, or whether the politically stimulated expansion is not in fact achieving the opposite of what it was originally intended to achieve, in other words, whether it is leading to the progressive redundancy of labour power itself:

> The process can be summarized as follows: created demand will lead to purchases of highly efficient and productive machine systems that need few men to control them: i.e. the installation of cybernation. Thus, in the relatively near future, a policy of forcing rapid growth in demand in order to increase employment opportunities will actually lead to the opposite result: it will raise unemployment rather than lower it.[8]

Some authors have drawn political conclusions from this argument that the full employment of the total social labour power is now no longer attainable. They have proposed the official elimination of the institutionalized, achievement-society-based principle of 'income through work'. In the USA in particular, the contemporary problem of those sections of the population which are in fact debarred from entering the labour market (the 'unemployables'),

[8] *Ibid.*, 90.

and which are therefore economically impoverished and socially
virtually unintegrable, apparently makes acceptable solutions that,
in principle, make access to use values* and position in the production process independent of one another. The introduction of the
'guaranteed income' demanded from various quarters[9] would achieve
this separation, since income would not then be dependent on work;
in reaction to the imperatives of economic stability, a model of
distribution is being proposed which would in fact further the
movement towards a society in which scarcity is abolished. Certainly
in its usual form the model is a watered down technocratic version,
since access to use values is seen as remaining tied to the money
form.

J. and M. Rowntree's analysis[10] shows that forgoing such solutions would not only heighten problems of poverty, but also rapidly
extend that type of repression which is not characterized any longer
by exploitation, but by the simple redundancy of labour power
and its mere subsumption under control in unproductive uses. The
authors give as examples the military apparatus and, with rather
more dubious justification, the education and training systems,
because in their labour economies function these merely *tie up*
labour power and squander it in unproductive intellectual training.
The authors omit to point out those functions of the *leisure industry*
in which 'free time' is absorbed and controlled without any productive or reproductive purpose for the economy.

In these three areas, conditions of deprivation and forms of control
are being created in which the conflict potential can no longer
be contained by appealing to the principle of achievement-based
remuneration. Many of the 'marginal group conflicts' which we
are witnessing today in the developed capitalist societies can be very
satisfactorily interpreted as the result of a 'legitimation vacuum',[11]
a vacuum created by the obsolescence of the principles of distribution according to equal exchange. The concessions mentioned above

* In *Capital* Marx distinguishes between exchange value (the quantitative
rate at which one commodity is exchanged against another) and use value
(the actual qualitative usefulness of the commodity to those who finally
consume it). (*Trans.*)

[9] Cf. *The triple revolution: manifesto of the ad hoc committee on the triple revolution*
(Santa Barbara 1964), and Theobald, *The guaranteed income.*

[10] J. and M. Rowntree, 'Youth as a class', *Int. Soc. J.* 5 (1968), 25–59;
Baran and Sweezy develop the concept of 'surplus' production in an analysis
of the system problems of advanced capitalist societies: see P. A. Baran
and P. M. Sweezy, *Monopoly capital* (New York 1966).

[11] The arguments in this introduction are organized around the problems
of the need for legitimacy and the legitimating ability of historical social
formations, as discussed in J. Habermas, *Technik und Wissenschaft als
'Ideologie'?* (Frankfurt a.M. 1968); English translation, 'Science and
technology as "ideology" ', in Habermas, *Knowledge and human interests*
(London 1972).

are intended to achieve political stability, yet they contain as much potential for social transformation as the conflicts they are intended to subdue. The concessions also propose a far-reaching revision of the dominant mode of distribution in the direction of a guaranteed income. If this were done, one of the basic assumptions of any mode of production based on wage labour would be abandoned.

This introduction began by outlining the thesis that the notion of the achieving society is an ideological and legitimating concept which is no longer adequate as a justificatory schema for complete industrial social structures. The thesis would seem to have been confirmed by the three developments which have been outlined (and unfortunately here could only be outlined): the displacement of initiative functions from privileged status groups to anonymous decision-making centres; the replacement of market-based guiding mechanisms by the administrative application of state power; the loss by growing sections of the total social labour force of their immediate link with the sphere of production, so that they are either maintained by a form of distribution independent of their performance or confronted with more or less naked pauperism.

At the same time, however, as the result of increasing interdependence and 'accident proneness' of the formally politicized system, there is a growing need for reliable integrative mechanisms: an affirmative congeniality traversing all subsystems and social groups becomes a condition of stability.[12] It would be possible to trace this dynamic contradiction at a macrosociological level and make it the starting point of a theory of crisis and conflict which, unlike economistic theories, included the level of legitimacy in the analysis. The present study, however, takes another path: it is an exclusively microsociological analysis of those mechanisms which *prevent* the system problem I have mentioned (the greater need for legitimacy combined with a smaller supply of justificatory schemas compatible with the existing social structure) becoming explicit and reaching crisis level. Initially the study assumes that a *routinized achievement principle* has a role in the affirmative consolidation of late capitalist and also of other highly industrialized social systems, a role which could be fulfilled by no other (comparatively rational) ideological system. Primary and secondary socialization form a style of life and work the origin of which in the social-philosophical and ideological model of the achieving society is no longer apparent: the ideology infiltrates the level of behaviour and there solidifies into a schema which is immune from all criticism. This obscures the historical limits of the conditions under which the achievement principle can become the organizing

[12] Cf. also C. Offe, 'Politische Herrschaft und Klassenstrukturen', in G. Kress and D. Senghaas (eds.), *Politikwissenschaft* (Frankfurt a.M. 1969), 155–89.

principle of a labour economy based upon equal exchange. In this study these conditions will be explicated, if not completely empirically, then certainly with empirically-based arguments and with empirical intention.

The study was finished in summer 1967. It was submitted as a dissertation to the Faculty of Social and Economic Sciences of the Johann-Wolfgang-Goethe University of Frankfurt.

Claus Offe

Frankfurt/Main, July 1969

I

The theoretical framework

Several broad trends can be deduced from general theories of the development of industrial work in technologically advanced societies. This study is not intended to be an investigation of these predictions; rather it will use them as the basis on which to form further hypotheses. Of the generally accepted assumptions of these theories the following are important for our purposes:

1   Industrial work is becoming increasingly 'separated from nature', in regard both to the composition of the labour force as a whole and to the structure of the individual workplace. Firstly, less and less work is merely the exploitation of natural elements, as in agriculture and the raw material industries, and this is clearly confirmed by the declining proportion of the labour force employed in those industries. Secondly, there is a diminishing demand for immediately natural human qualities such as physical strength, natural skills etc.

2   A series of technical instruments have been interposed between the worker and the material on which he works. The purposeful use of these instruments presupposes a series of educational and training processes. As the direct confrontation with nature in the work process declines, so the importance of the training processes increases, so that to a growing extent they comprise the ability to work itself.

This situation is normally discussed in terms of the concept of 'specialization', a concept which refers both to the increasing division of labour, documented in the permanently increasing number of job definitions, *and* to the growth of educational and training processes which prepare the individual to carry out specialized occupational functions.

However, it is debatable whether industrial work is in fact developing in such a way that it can be assumed that training requirements are growing to an equal extent for all jobs.[1] While in some sectors there is a trend towards increasing qualifications,

[1] Cf. F. Pollock, *Automation* (Frankfurt a.M. 1964); W. Siebel, 'Berufs-qualifikation im automatisierten Industrie-betrieb', in *Soziale Welt* 15 (4) (1964).

this has to be set against the disqualification of some other jobs. While there has been assumed to be a trend towards an overall increase in both the division of labour and qualifications, the reality is in fact rather more ambiguous. It follows that the concept of specialization itself has to be defined more precisely. First of all, 'specialization' has to be made independent of the mere *extent* of the training process. This also seems desirable since the institutionalized training requirements of a particular job are not necessarily a reliable indicator of the actual requirements of work in the job. In addition many of the qualifications that actually are required are only gained in the workplace itself. In this study, then, specialization will be conceived not as the increases in the extent of the necessary qualifications linked to a job position, but rather the increasing *difference* between the requirements operating at one position and those at another position. Therefore the empirical criterion for specialization is the 'non-transferability' of job qualifications to use in other jobs: specialization is the non-liquidity of the individual labour investment. The longer the preparatory and retraining period needed for the acquisition of full functional ability in an alternative job position, the lower the transferability. This dimension—the transferability of qualifications *between* jobs—cuts across the dimension of qualification *at* the job, and it is in terms of the first dimension that all job positions can be assumed to be becoming increasingly specialized.

3   Taken together with the proven growth in the size of industrial production and administrative organizations, these training and specialization processes have an important consequence for the organizational system of advanced industrial firms and bureaucracies. Parallel to the 'hierarchical' ranking of positions in an organization, there emerges the new organizational principle of 'functional differentiation'.[2] Hierarchical differentiation and functional differentiation both produce status systems, and in the course of industrial development these two systems become independent of one another. This can be seen in the fact that in industry, trade, administration and also in the military it is becoming increasingly unlikely that people with the same status inside the organization will have the same functional tasks to fulfil. Conversely, it is increasingly likely that a single task will be carried out by means of the cooperation of different ranks in the organization. This is different to pre-industrial and early industrial forms of work organization, where it was possible to assume a widespread identity of function and status. In industrial societies, on the other hand, the tendency is for it to be impossible to represent the hierarchical status system of an industrial or administrative organization in terms of a technical or functional continuum.

[2] R. Dahrendorf, *Industrie- und Betriebssoziologie* (Berlin 1965).

The argument can be clarified by introducing the concept of the *task-continuous status organization* (in which functional and hierarchical differentiation coincide) and opposing to it the concept of the *task-discontinuous status organization*. The following contrasts the two structural types as organizational models.

In the continuous type of status organization the positions (A, B, C) are ranked one above the other and authorized orders pass downwards from one position to another. The relationship between the positions is such that there is a wide area of technical rules to which equal obedience is required from all the occupants of the positions (Pa, Pb, Pc). Position B differs from its subordinate position C merely in that it is defined in terms of greater mastery of the rules and greater ability, knowledge and experience in production. Thus the rules which Pc must obey become in their entirety (or very nearly so) components of the role definition of Pb. Similarly, the same applies to the relationship of A to B, so the highest position in a hierarchy includes the basic requirements which are placed on the most subordinate position. Simplifying slightly, this structural type can perhaps be said to be represented in the production organization of the small craft workshop, with its triple hierarchical division of master, journeyman and apprentice.

This structural type should be contrasted to the other type, that of the task-discontinuous status organization. In this case the relationship between the hierarchically ordered positions is such that the mastery of the technical rules of position C is basically *not* an essential component of position B. In position B, the requirements of position C are replaced by other aspects of the work role, which are acquired, or maybe even must be acquired, in other ways than through the previous occupation of position C. In other words, functional differentiation has occurred. A well-known example of this process of functional differentiation and the new structural type that results from it is the relationship of foreman, chargehand and production worker. The task areas of these positions and the technical knowledge and abilities required for their fulfilment no longer coincide: at any rate there is not the smallest element of the role definition of the lowest member of the organization's status hierarchy which is common to all the other positions.

This second structural type of organization, that of the task-discontinuous status organization with its non-identity of hierarchical and functional organization, is becoming more and more predominant. This can be confirmed empirically by the results of the many studies of the job definitions of chargehands, foremen and middle management.

The difference between the two organizational types is shown schematically in figure 1. The shaded areas designate the area of the work role in which the knowledge, ability and experience

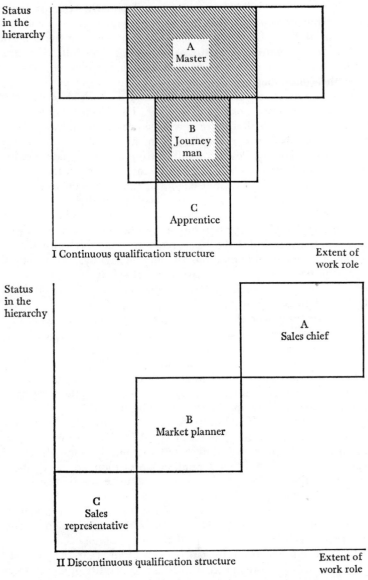

FIG. 1. Task-continuous and task-discontinuous status organizations.

required at one position coincide with that which makes up the qualification of the subordinate position.

The structural type of task-discontinuous status organization brings heterogeneous qualifications and work functions into an order of vertical rank. This results in a relationship between 'below' and 'above' such that some of the decisions that have to be made in the lower position are not fully covered by the commands and controls from above—they therefore have to be left to the independent decision of the workers.

Herbert A. Simon has used this point to analyse formal organizations and to investigate the extent of discretion possible in different positions.[3]

> Influence is exercised in the most complete form when a decision promulgated by one person governs every aspect of the behavior of another. On the parade ground, the marching soldier is permitted no discretion whatsoever. . . . Most often, organizational influences place only partial limits upon the exercise of discretion.[4]

The change from full to fragmentary control can be seen most clearly in the military sector:

> In ancient warfare, the battlefield was not unlike the parade-ground. An entire army was often commanded by a single man, and his authority extended in a very complete and direct form to the lowest man in the ranks. This was possible because the entire battlefield was within range of a man's voice and because tactics were for the most part executed by the entire army in unison.[5]

The comparison of the warfare of antiquity with the organizational form of contemporary military units makes clear therefore the preconditions for extensive formal control:

1   The vertical (hierarchical) differentiation must be relatively undeveloped, thus allowing the direct communication of orders and direct supervision of their execution.

2   The events and processes in the sphere of action have to occur within the field of vision and within hearing distance of the superior authorities.

3   Functional differentiation must also be rudimentary: not only must the majority of the actors belong to the same rank in the hierarchy, but also actors of the same rank must fulfil identical functions.

This differentiation of the two structural types makes a further analytical differentiation possible, based on the classification of the rules contained in the job role that have to be followed by the occupant of the position. A job role is defined as the totality of the rules linked to a specific workplace or to a specific task, while the role itself is constituted by sanctioned and institutionalized expectations. Usually the expectations which make up the rules are not

---

[3] H. A. Simon, 'Decision making and administrative organization', in R. K. Merton *et al.* (eds.), *Reader in bureaucracy* (New York 1952), 185–94.
[4] *Ibid.*, 186–7.
[5] *Ibid.*, 188.

themselves classified any further, with the result that no account is taken of the special structural aspects of different rules. However, such a differentiation is necessary for an analysis of the achievement principle, for the achievement principle clearly has to do with the extent of the fulfilment of the rules specific to the work situation.

Simon implies that certain conditions are necessary for *direct* control. If these conditions are no longer fulfilled, then formal control has to be replaced by functional equivalents which derive from outside the formal authority structure. In general it is true that:

> The broader the sphere of discretion left to the subordinate by the orders given him, the more important become these types of influence which do not depend upon the exercise of formal authority.[6]

Functionally equivalent forms of control consist of 'organizational loyalties', 'striving towards efficient forms of action', informal controls and training. As both hierarchical and functional differentiation proceeds, the compliance which results from the effects of formal control has to be supplemented by *additional* normative orientations. Simon attaches the greatest importance here to the creation of institutional loyalties and to the emergence of routines and of habitual forms of action :

> The phenomenon of identification, or institutional loyalty, performs a very important function in administration.[7] Training, as a mode of influence upon decisions, has its greatest value in those situations where the exercise of formal authority through command proves difficult. The difficulty may lie in the need for prompt action, in the spatial dispersion of the organization, or in the complexity of the subject matter of decisions, which defies summarization in rules and regulations.[8]

If it is not backed by these other means of control,

> authority is relatively important to control decision in any but a negative way. The elements entering in all but the most routine decisions are so numerous and so complex that it is impossible to control positively more than a few. Unless a subordinate is himself able to supply most of the premises of decision, and to synthesize them adequately, the task of supervision becomes hopelessly burdensome.[9]

Thus, in this type of multirank hierarchical system the relevant abilities (technical knowledge, etc.) are not distributed *cumulatively*. As a result the higher authority *cannot* have a monopoly of the definition either of the work goals or of the technical rules that specify how these goals are to be achieved. The subordinate positions in the hierarchy are now work positions which are not directly

[6] *Ibid.*, 189.
[7] *Ibid.*, 190.
[8] *Ibid.*, 193.
[9] *Ibid.*

'transparent' all the time to those above them: the possibility of external control has been reduced. In this situation, if the organization's goals are to be carried out it is a *functional necessity* that this loss of *external* control is compensated for by *internal* controls, i.e. the individual must now himself interpret the goals and carry them out independently. An organization of this sort can only exist if *an internal system of goal-oriented decision-making rules and action orientations* and a normative commitment of the worker replaces the detailed hierarchical controls of the craft workshop type of unit—in which work tasks can be fulfilled merely by following the necessary *technical rules*.

Inside the organization, instructions to subordinate authorities change their form, a change which could possibly even be traced in their changing linguistic structure. Instructions no longer refer to a course of action of which every separate phase is comprehensible, predictable and controllable from 'above' and the achievement of which is exclusively dependent on the necessary productive ability and knowledge. Instead, instructions now refer much more to the desired *results* of courses of action. As far as the separate phases of their execution are concerned, orders necessarily include 'discretion' and room for interpretation, so that the subordinates *must* develop their own complimentary goal interpretations and their own independent commitment if the planned result is to be achieved.

This automatic knowledge of the correct premises of action is a necessary basic qualification that appears for the first time in task-discontinuous organizations with their discontinuous vertical authority relations. This fact allows us to differentiate between two classes of rules from which the work role is made up.

1   Technical rules of behaviour or procedure: under this heading should be understood the totality of physical productive ability, and of the productive knowledge and ability gained through experience and practice, i.e. all that is necessary at a specific workplace in order to carry out the relevant task.
2   Normative orientation: by this is meant all the norms, values, interests and motives which it is expected will be obeyed within the institutional structure of the work process.

Within the area of normative orientations we have to make a further differentiation. There are (a) rules which are distinguished from the *technical* role elements, in that their applicability is not limited to one particular set of work functions at one specific workplace, but which nevertheless do contribute to the functioning of the structure of cooperative action which makes up the work process. Examples are such norms as carefulness, economy etc. These rules, which are not specific to the work situation but which operate within it, I will term *regulative norms*. In addition there is (b) the other group of normative orientations, which are certainly empirically assumed or expected to be followed in the work situation, yet which nonetheless make absolutely no functional contribution to the work procedure, and, as a purely ideological component of the work role, simply prop up the authority structure of the organization. Examples are the acceptance of the norms of an occupational culture, loyalty to the aims and interests of people in authority, etc. This type of normative orientation will be termed here *extrafunctional orientations*.

Differentiating between these types of rules allows us to construct a continuum of the elements of the job role between two poles, that of *functionality* for the work task ('technical rules') and of *functional* irrelevance for the work task. In the middle, between the two poles, lies the category of regulatory norms. These are characterized by the fact that in their *objective* function they allow, or at least facilitate, the operation of the cooperative work process. The nearer the hierarchical work organization approaches the task-discontinuous type, the more important such regulatory norms become. However, adherence to regulatory norms is not experienced by the actors as being instrumental to the achievement of work tasks. Rather, orientation to these rules derives from areas of life outside work, so that in the consciousness of the actors themselves there is no deliberate functional connection between the rules and the work task. This aspect of the rules applies also to extrafunctional orientations: all normative orientations are experienced by the actors as unrelated to their work.

At the moment we are concerned only with the analytical aspects of this differentiation and not with its operation. The range of the elements of the work roles can be illustrated by a diagram:

	Technical rules	Regulatory norms	Extrafunctional orientatiolns
Objective function in the fulfilment of the work task	Functional	Functional	Functionaly irrelevant
Subjective orientation	Instrumental	Non-instrumental	Non-instrumental

Normative orientations

The trend of development that is assumed to exist for industrial and bureaucratic work can now be described as a movement from a model of organizational work in terms of continuous qualification structures towards the other pole of discontinuous (but still hierarchical) structures. This is paralleled by a relaxing of the restrictions on individual discretion: to an increasing extent it becomes functionally necessary that external controls are replaced with internal regulations. In addition, a parallel social change occurs at the level of the work organization and at the level of the composition of the work roles.

Such a social change, occurring equally across industrial, administrative and military organizations, affects organizations at the core of their authority structure, their stratification system and their internal processes of social mobility. Namely, in a situation in which the combination of the subordinate's ability to produce and the superior's rights of command and punishment no longer suffice to ensure the fulfilment of work functions, the foundations are removed from mechanisms of status distribution as they are conceived in the normative model of the achieving society (see chapter 2). The possession of knowledge and ability directly related to performance is still necessary, but now the category of normative rules becomes a further functional precondition for participation in the work process. To the extent that this occurs, the categories of individual performance become useless as a means of determining individual status.

At its most general, the content of normative orientations which operate as rules for action and decision-making in the organization consists of a generalized work ethic that includes such virtues as hard work, punctuality, economy, carefulness, perseverance, exactitude etc.[10] A further stage towards the pole of extrafunctional orientations is comprised by the knowledge of and conformity to the attitudes and values of superiors, co-workers and subordinates. Finally, a still more extreme form of these extrafunctional orientations occurs when the individual internalizes these end goals and submits to the criteria which derive from a dominant system of values and interests.

The prescriptive model of the achieving society presents status as being distributed according to the characteristics of activity which are part of the *work* component of the job role. *So long as this is in fact the case*, the different types of rules which can function as components of the work role are differentially suitable for determining the status of individuals. In work roles which are defined exclusively by the categories of performance-related knowledge and ability, ascribing differential status to individuals according to the characteristics of their work activity presents no problem. However, in job roles which also require normative orientations, because they are defined within the framework of a task-discontinuous work organization, the greater the proportion of the role that is comprised by these normative orientations, the more difficult it is to differentiate between individuals. There are in fact four reasons

[10] Cf. R. Dahrendorf, 'Industrielle Fertigkeiten und soziale Schichtung', *KZfSS* 8 (1956), 540–68.

why normative orientations cannot operate as the measure of individual status:

1   According to the normative model of the achieving society, the individual's performance-related abilities can be interpreted along the lines of private property, yet in the case of normative orientations this is impossible. Norms arise through a process of cultural interaction—in the family, in the school, in peer-groups etc.—and are therefore not personality characteristics but rather supra-individual rules of collectivities and institutions. Where individual status is distributed according to obedience to normative orientations, the determinants of status are not individual characteristics such as performance-related knowledge and ability, physical strength, intelligence and technical experience, but rather the membership of institutions, collectivities and subcultures.

2   Unlike technical rules of procedure, norms cannot be clearly pictured as lying along a continuum according to their relative value. Norms arise through a dialogue within socialization agencies. This way in which they are created corresponds to their relationship to each other: it is a relationship which in no way (not even in terms of the subjective 'costs' of the creation of norms) can plausibly be pictured as one of a rank order, but which can only be understood as the coexistence of different forms of life that are in principle all of equal value. For example, according to whether the work situation has to do predominantly with things, with symbols or with people, so a different system of regulative norms will be applied, and these normative systems can no longer (not even from a functional point of view) be fitted into an evaluative rank order. Unlike the case of individual performance ability and status, a correlation between the norms that are obeyed and individual status becomes categorically inappropriate. This applies because in the case of obedience to norms, status distribution does not occur (as the achievement principle lays down it should) according to characteristics of individuals' activity in work, but rather according to the extent of their conformity with a dominant normative system. The perhaps previously rational legitimation of status through performance is now transformed into discrimination against or favouring of particular cultural groups. Furthermore, completely extra-functional criteria, such as group membership and ascribed status, can replace rational rules of status distribution and completely dissolve the rational connection between characteristics of the individual's work and his or her individual status.

3   A further difference between norms and technical rules of procedure is that complex organizations can increasingly only do without normative identifications and institutional loyalties at the cost of a complete breakdown. Yet these normative elements are

not only acquired without any subjective costs, they also differ from rules of performance ability in that in a certain sense obeying them does not have any positive ('initiatory') influence on the results of the work being carried out.

Above all, such orientative norms have a double function. They *prevent* deviation from the 'intended' goal of work which is laid down in advance[11] and they also ward off conflicts. Since the work procedures themselves are so complex that a successful outcome cannot be fully guaranteed through a system of formal rules and direct supervisory control, goals and means which lead to the 'one best way' of carrying out the work have to be chosen autonomously, and this choice is a question of avoiding errors, more costly alternatives, breakdowns and social conflicts. Following norms which prescribe the 'right' behaviour serves more to safeguard the prescribed result than to enable the individual to determine the level of output; from the point of view also of business administration and technology, in mechanized production the main aim is seen as being to minimize faulty behaviour and its consequence while maintaining a given level of output (rather than to maximize output by fully utilizing all the factors of production). The most important consequence is that also *within* a status group that is concerned with technically and organizationally similar tasks, the possibility disappears of any rational grading of the members according to measures of performances or by the judgements of their superiors. While in the achieving society model with its hierarchies based on performance, it was a question of an individualistic competition based on criteria of performance and on technical-intellectual abilities, such that in principle an infinitely fine grading of the status scale was possible, now the possibility of a rational classification collapses into a dichotomy: either the person *has* the normative controls, in which case the value of his activity does not differ from that of others in any way at all, or such controls do *not* function, so the dysfunctions already discussed emerge and cause the person to leave the relevant functional status group (or, alternatively, the socialization process which should have transferred these norms and motives is rectified). The only chance of a rational status classi-

[11] This suggests a comparison with a similar structural change in the legal system: the classical concept of law entailed a precise definition of the contents and consequences of each law, thus allowing neither the judge nor the citizen much room for any interpretation or evaluation. However, the legal system now includes general clauses (e.g. as contained in such formulations as 'law and order', 'truth and honesty', 'each has to act, such that . . .', 'bearing in mind all the circumstances . . .'). Once this occurs, then the legal system can only fulfil its function of arbitrating social conflict to the extent that normative preconceptions and interpretive schemas provide citizens and judges with a clear operationalization of those legal phrases the meaning of which is left open by the way they are formulated.

fication then remains measuring the economic losses caused by the deviant behaviour or the benefits which this behaviour caused to be forgone (always assuming the possibility that 'dysfunctions' can still be attributed to particular individuals). Such an evaluation of the results of *omissions* and of deviant behaviour is exactly what is implied in the notion of 'responsibility', a notion which is increasingly receiving more attention for judging the value of positions and of individual employees. However, it is clear that the extent of the 'damage' which results in such cases can in no way be understood as a characteristic which determines the status of individuals: rather the damage has to be traced back to the technical and organizational conditions of work which allocate differentially high (economic) risks to different positions *independently* of the individuals who occupy them. Here, although the criterion of responsibility is being applied, there is still a deviation from what the achieving society prescribes, since it is not the productive value of the individual's behaviour which is being measured, but rather the possible disturbances or losses which would occur with the non-occurrence of a particular action. In addition, a quality such as responsibility or risk tolerance obviously cannot be placed on a par with categories of performance ability, since it is one of the class of regulative norms that are acquired in primary or secondary socialization processes.

4   A final difference between normative rules and those of performance ability is the fact that the following of norms is not as stable as the application of technical rules can be assumed to be. While knowledge and ability must be taken to be comparatively invariable personality attributes, obedience to norms and the maintainance of loyalty, although certainly broadly determined by socialization processes, are nonetheless in part open to reflexive alteration and modification.

Only to the extent that both the set of reciprocal expectations within a set of reference groups *and* the self-interpretation and self-understanding of the role partners remain constant can any long-term maintainance of the norms be assumed, and these norms now have to control in an ad hoc fashion the area of discretion that is no longer covered by formal rules. Power conflicts within the organization, relative deprivation and informal conflicts thus affect the functional ability of a structure of division of labour far more than is assumed in the achieving society model. Once again it is clear that the wider social structure determines what rules are followed at work, and that any attempt to evaluate performance in individualistic terms must end up disguising the social origins of the rules themselves.

Earlier we deduced the growing importance of normative orientations in the work role from the changes in the structure of work organizations. Before we can discover how far this assumption is also valid as far as the technological characteristics of modern production are concerned, we have at this stage to discuss one possible counter-argument—the thesis that the importance of motivational and normative orientations does not increase with the development of labour technology, but rather *declines*.

The literature of industrial sociology sometimes distinguishes between three factors which influence or control work behaviour, allocating them to corresponding authorities by whom the control is exercised. Such a choice of control factors appears roughly as follows:

1   *Economic* control: this is exercised by the supervisory functions of the immediate superior (foreman etc.). The function of control is to stabilize costs and output at the required level.

2   *Normative* control: this is usually seen as deriving from the informal groups in the factory, which for their part standardize the output at a 'suitable' level and ensure that this level is kept to by the workers.

3   *Technical* control: the 'subject' of this control is the technical equipment, which through its mere functioning, and the obvious results connected to this, exercises a constraining pressure on performance, thus taking over the controls which, with highly mechanized equipment, can no longer be applied by the first form of control.

Roughly, the arguments summarized by the phrase 'the transformation of personal into technological control' are as follows: in earlier stages of technology and of work organization the control of the functionally correct work behaviour was reserved for personal and competent supervision by the foreman and similar persons in authority. In the 'supervisory' type of work (i.e. the mere inspection of the functioning of highly mechanized equipment), as already in the intermediate stages of 'mechanized' work, the starting point of control moves more and more to the machine itself, which has a regular operation that provokes almost sportive motivation and leads to work becoming habitual behaviour. In this way, so it is claimed, not only is the controlling authority displaced, but also the absolute level of the necessary controls changes, precisely because in the process of the changing of the work conditions the dominant *sort* of strain changes. Physical strain, which leads to strong opposition to it and which has to be overcome by correspondingly tight controls, declines in favour of mental and nervous strain, which is easier to put up with and which can therefore be stabilized by milder controls.

Clearly such an approach cannot be reconciled with the hypothesis that has been formulated here, namely that a *growth* in the functioning of normative control ('regulatory norms') is a result of technological changes in the work situation. The opposition between 'technical' and 'normative' controls can only be overcome when one attempts to trace the concept of technical control itself back to normative elements.

Certainly, it is in no way clear how the personnel supervisory functions of earlier stages of technology and work organization could now suddenly be taken over by self-evident and autonomously operating machine processes (as the argument sketched above claims is the case). If this did occur, then it would roughly mean that a worker who faces a part passing by on an assembly line has factually *no* alternative course of action open to him, other than to carry out the procedure prescribed to him at his workplace. Mechanized work procedure has taken from him every influence on the product, so that stabilizing his work behaviour need rely neither on external and personal nor on internal and normative controls.

The weakness of this argument becomes obvious when one makes Lutz and Willener's distinction between 'initiatory' and 'preventive' influence on the work process:[12] in this imaginary assembly-line situation it is true that the worker has only a small amount of 'initiatory' influence (i.e. he cannot determine the workspeed, the quality of the product, the material, the production procedures or the amount of output). However, what does remain open to him is the possibility of 'omissive action'. While, as individual, he cannot modify, alter or overfulfil the regulations which make up his work role, he can at any time omit or even refuse to fulfil one or all of these norms. Thus, even with the strictest shaping by technology of the work procedures and the relationships of cooperation, the worker always has the opportunity to make mistakes, to produce rejects, to work carelessly, to create dysfunctional conflicts in the structure of cooperation and to 'fail' in every possible way.[13]

There are even factors which suggest that the more the functions and the hierarchical organization diverge, and the more the labour technology develops, the more important internal control becomes:

I   In horizontally differentiated relationships of dependency, in

[12] B. Lutz and A. Willener, *Mechanisierungsgrad und Entlohnungsform: Zusammenfassender Bericht* (Luxemburg 1959).

[13] Lutz and Willener's distinction between initiatory and preventive influence can be paralleled by a conceptual distinction mentioned briefly by Stinchcombe ('Some empirical consequences of the Davis-Moore theory of stratification', in R. Bendix and S. M. Lipset (eds.), *Class, status and power* (2nd edn, New York 1966), 69–73). He distinguishes between enterprises in which a qualification has a 'complementary' character in relation to physical production and to fellow workers (i.e. the employment of a more talented worker leads to a disproportionate increase in the value of the product—*translator's note*) and those enterprises in which qualifications have merely 'additive' effects.

which not every stage of the cooperative work is hierarchically controllable, very small omissions can have serious results, particularly with highly capital-intensive production.

2   Such omissions are less easy to punish or sanction effectively in those situations in which it is difficult for a decentralized system of supervision to find the 'guilty' person and bring him to account.

3   The cause of failure of a complete production system composed of men together with machines can just as well be the failure of technical elements as human error. In every concrete case the question of responsibility can only adequately be decided by those people in the organizational hierarchy who have the same technical knowledge and experience that exists at the level where the failure occurred. However, in task-discontinuous organizations the immediate supervisor usually cannot fulfil this condition of technical competence, so it is possible to disguise deviant behaviour as 'technical trouble'.

Frequently, too, the concept of 'preventive' influence provides the option of not taking independent action. While the working individual is certainly able to see, although in an ad hoc way, that action is needed to prevent breakdowns occurring, this necessary action is not contained in any formal work regulation and therefore has not been made part of the formal work role: in a situation such as this there is simply no legitimate way in which omissions can be punished.

Lutz and Willener have demonstrated this difference between preventive and initiatory influence in their comparative study of several steelrolling mills. In the same study they also show the validity of the thesis of the growth of 'preventive' influence:

> In a modern rolling mill it is more important that the regulations are carried out without the slightest error than that a few more tonnes are produced.[14]
>
> It is one of the basic characteristics of the modern development of work that from a certain level of mechanization and modernization a new form of influence becomes visible: the worker may be very tightly locked into the different technical organizational and co-operative systems which now leave open to him only a small amount of independent influence. At first sight his intervention in the production process is completely pre-determined and devoid of any influence on it, nonetheless it is shaped by a very high level of 'preventive' influence.[15]

The argument, then, is that the reduction of direct and personal domination and surveillance, as occurs in technologically advanced working conditions, is not compensated for by technical controls alone; such a compensation can only work when additional normative orientations become effective in the working individual.

[14] Lutz and Willener, *Mechanisierungsgrad und Entlohnungsform*, 97.
[15] *Ibid.*, 104.

Such a thesis is supported by the fact that an area of individual influence continues to exist and has even expanded. Certainly, this influence no longer takes a positive or initiatory form, but largely a preventive one. However, if this area of autonomous influence is to be used in the functionally correct way, mere technical rules are inadequate, while the now much relaxed network of personal supervision is equally ineffective: the gap in control that has developed now has to be filled by regulatory norms. Initiatory influence is a question of applying a particular set of technical rules of procedure within specific and constant external conditions and prohibitions. Preventive influence, on the other hand, is not used correctly merely by following general rules which can in principle be enforced by direct orders: *it is used functionally when the worker does not allow deviations, omission, mistakes, conflicts and any actions which would prevent the work tasks being fulfilled within a certain institutional framework.* The formal organization and the prescribed work procedures can never fully define and encapsulate such 'rules of avoidance': breaking them cannot be punished through a formalized system of penalties and of other means of coercion.

We have now located two reasons which lead us to expect normative orientations to make up a growing part of the work role.

1   The first reason is an organizational consequence of the discontinuous distribution of tasks: internalized rules become functionally necessary when the network of official hierarchical controls becomes looser and hence the level of direct supervision declines.

2   The second reason is a technological one. As the level of mechanization rises, so the worker's area of discretion grows. This area of discretion has to be utilized by the worker consciously and in conformity with the rules of the organization: he must have a normatively-based desire to do the 'right' thing at the right time, even when there is no official supervision and even with the decline in the risk that he will be held responsible for 'wrong' behaviour as it becomes more and more difficult to trace these causes of dysfunctions back to the behaviour of individuals.

Both these arguments lead to the same conclusion. In mechanized and hierarchical work organizations characterized by a specialized division of labour, it must be internalized controls that can ensure that tasks are carried out. For this reason, therefore, we can expect an increase in the normative part of the work role.

The following chapters will investigate the consequences of this structural change for the rational application of the achievement principle. These have in fact already been hinted at by Lutz and Willener:

Up to a certain stage in technological development the workers have a chance of direct influence on the speed of work, which could be designated as initiatory influence: their contribution to the results of production can be measured because and in so far as it varies quantitatively. The situation is different with technologically advanced equipment: here the worker only affects production *indirectly*, in that by following the operation instructions he prevents a reduction of the normal performance of the production system ('preventive' influence). The worker no longer has the choice of producing more or less, but only the possibility of doing the right or the wrong thing. His contribution now varies only qualitatively.[16]

The conceptual distinctions introduced up to this point in the study can now be summarized:

Technological level	'Near to nature' non-specialized preconditions for work	'Separated from nature' processes of education and specialization
Corresponding type of hierarchical structure	Task - continuous, hierarchical and functional organization identical, orders are technical instructions	Task-discontinuous, hierarchical and functional organization diverges, orders partly require interpretation
Corresponding type of control	External force, normative involvement is unnecessary	Normative involvement at a premium, secondary socialization processes
Type of influence	Initiatory	Preventive

[16] *Ibid.*, 113.

2

The concept of the achieving society

The concept of the achieving society is laden with normative content which extends beyond its merely descriptive form. To this extent the concept does not really belong in sociological terminology and, at least in Germany, this ambivalence between prescription and description has prevented it being used in scientific work. More than almost any other typological concept within sociology, it unites elements of description with an evaluative self-intepretation of an overall social structure. However, the concept is frequently used in pre- and semi-scientific commentaries, where it is used as a universal legitimating principle through which a particular part of the social structure is criticized and assessed. If we start from these pre-scientific self-interpretations of industrial societies (and certainly not just of capitalist industrial societies) and define the concept more clearly, we do not gain any description of the real social structure; instead, we get a description of the most important status-legitimating principle that these societies accept as valid and even claim to fulfil. The 'achieving society' has then to be understood as merely one model of the social processes determining and sanctioning individual status, a model that has been elevated into a norm and institutionalized in a whole series of ways.

If a society understands itself as an achieving society, it makes one particular mechanism of status distribution into the norm. Kluth describes this normative model of the achieving society as follows:

> In industrial society, under the cover of a pluralism of values, a sort of value monism is beginning to prevail. It seems at least that in industrial societies 'performance' is in no way just a regulatory and distributive norm for economic work, but rather that it is becoming more and more the value principle that regulates all areas of life. One could say ... that performance is well on the way to becoming the only over-arching value category in industrial societies. The quantity and quality of work is seen in terms of amounts of performance; the material and social opportunities of the society are supposed to be distributed according to standards of individual performance, as is the recognition and the prestige that a person is allowed to claim and to expect. The bourgeois industrial world with its anti-caste outlook immediately makes every

social claim appear questionable and unjust which is not at least in principle based on quantifiable performance. Performance thus counts ... as the single legitimate measure of every form of social honour. This immediately presupposes the belief that everything humans do is measurable and thus objectively ascertainable. For example, the many attempts to make everything that humans do in work measurable and thus objectively comparable as 'quantitative amounts' all rest upon this belief. In industrial society [there is] an ideal according to which all performance is the exact expression of an equivalent.[1]

The model of distribution contained in the idea of the achieving society is remarkable for its peculiar ambivalence. Its social and political intention doubtless derives from the tradition of egalitarian thought: it challenges all social privileges and all caste-type barriers to social mobility that cannot be functionally justified; in addition it aims at the extensive development of the forces of human productivity and of industrial welfare; finally it strives for an explicitly individualistic form of social status distribution, since the individual is meant to be the only reference point for distribution processes. The works of Saint Simon bring together these aims for the first time into a utopian model of society.

On the other hand the achievement principle does not operate merely as a norm which ensures equality, but just as much also as a legitimating principle to justify social inequality—it restricts social inequality in the very moment that it propagates a claim for it.[2] The achievement principle sanctions those forms of inequality which have resulted from individual achievement and in this way it is *also* a norm of inequality.

Above all in capitalist industrial societies, the importance of the achievement principle results in part from this second function, that of legitimating inequality. The striking differences in material and non-material life-chances that occur in social structures need some form of explanatory justification and, given the egalitarian premises of the system, such a justification cannot any longer be derived from pre-industrial forms of legitimating status distribution. The achievement principle is also of great functional importance because in industrial societies a large and growing proportion of the work process is carried out in only indirect contact with the market: the typical form of work is one enclosed within an organized social institution. While the early liberal form of capitalism ensured a continual direct evaluation of the individual work of the commodity producers by means of market prices, the growth of large-scale organizational forms of work means an at least temporary exclusion of the working individual from the evaluative mechanisms

---

[1] H. Kluth, 'Amtsgedanke und Pflichtethos in der Industriegesellschaft', *Hmb. Jb.* 10 (1965), 11–22, here 18.
[2] A fact criticized by Marx. Cf. 'Critique of the Gotha programme', in Marx and Engels, *Selected works* (3 vols., Moscow 1970) III, 9–30.

of the market.[3] Thus the value relationships of performance which were previously represented by market-price relationships now have to be located and made the basis of status distribution *independently* of the market. This occurs through a concept of performance which makes it ascertainable independently of its price. It is in this way that one can explain the particular relevance of the idea of performance in the evaluation of work in *organized* social institutions.

By drawing on labour and business administration literature, together with the model of the achieving society on which it is based, we can outline the core of this model. The achieving society is based on the general rule that the social status of an individual is supposed to depend upon his status in the sphere of work and production, while in turn his status within the hierarchical organizations of the production sphere is meant to depend on his individual performance.

An operational definition of the model's dependent variable, social status, is institutionalized with work organizations. This definition is comprised of those status dimensions through which the organizations themselves define the position of an individual within a hierarchical system. Apart from symbolic and 'non-material' rewards, which will not be discussed here, these dimensions are basically the following four:

admission to occupational position (recruitment)
distribution of income gained from work
social mobility to a 'higher' position in the same organization
    (promotion)
receiving the power to give orders (formal authority).

Obviously the four status dimensions are not independent of one another, but usually vary together. In principle, however, it is possible for a person's status to change on one dimension while staying constant on the other three dimensions.

Listing these dimensions clarifies the 'dependent' side of the normative structure represented by the achievement principle. The principle therefore states that an individual can only be formally recruited to an occupational position, and/or receive a different income from his work, and/or be given a different work task within the same organization, and/or be granted formal authority when and only when he fulfils a standard of performance laid down by an objective criterion (i.e. one that is independent of the particular person).

Before we attempt to conceptualize the 'independent' dimension of achievement, there is one question that has to be clarified: we have to decide what are the real or alleged social functions which are claimed to follow from the realization of the achievement prin-

[3] F. Fürstenberg, *Probleme der Lohnstruktur* (Tübingen 1958).

ciple—functions which therefore give the achievement principle the character of a legitimate criterion of rank in societal labour and also in such areas as art and sport.

We can distinguish four functions allegedly fulfilled by the achievement principle. This will show why it is precisely those organizations in which status is dependent upon performance that lay claim to be the most 'just' and the most 'rational' form of organization.

1   *The compensatory function.* Working is assumed to entail either subjective or objective 'costs'. These costs can consist of the subjectively experienced effort at work or the stressful character of the working conditions. Alternatively, they can be the subjective and objective costs which are incurred by acquiring the level of productive ability and productive knowledge necessary to fulfil specific work tasks. This second category includes the costs of training and the gains that have to be forgone which would have been received if the labour power had been used in a different fashion. An organization where status depends upon performance has therefore the function of compensating the individual for the different subjective and objective costs, varying from worker to worker, which are incurred before or during work.

2   *The principle of equivalence.* Wherever status is made dependent on performance, this dependency has the additional function of making ascriptive payments impossible (i.e. status definition derived from sex, age, ethnic or regional background etc.): the principle of 'equal pay for equal work' thus prevents irrational discrimination. A status organization of this sort thus leads to a particular form of social equality.

3   *The productivity principle.* The achievement principle is considered to have the function of moderating social conflicts, for it removes exploitative relationships and distributes in a just fashion the results of labour. This function operates, so it is claimed, to the extent that the economically valuable results of the individual's labour only becomes controlled by others if the worker himself benefits. It is in this way that the wages theory of economics attempts to explain the level of the wage rate through the marginal productivity of labour.

4   *The allocative function.* Since the status dimensions that are controlled by the formal economic organizations are of such dramatic importance for the total living conditions of the workers, and since these organizations therefore determine the extent to which every individual can satisfy his desires, the application of the achievement principles has the function of transforming the pressure of the needs to which every individual is subjected into the maximum readiness to produce. Further, this willingness is therefore

distributed across the production process in such a way that the system as a whole reaches the optimum level of productivity. Both at the micro- and at the macro-economic level these mechanisms ensure the creation of an equilibrium at the point of optimal labour productivity. At a micro-economic level it is expected that in general the worker in a factory applies the maximum amount of energy to the fulfilment of his work tasks, so that this function of individual *incentive* helps to maximize productivity. At a micro-economic level the mechanisms of occupational choice and the labour market are supposed to ensure the most rational allocation and distribution of the labour factor of production. These two functions of the achievement principle can be brought together in the concept of the allocative function of the achievement principle.

As already stated, the legitimacy of the achievement principle is based on its claim to fulfil these four functions. If this claim is to be actually realized in practice, then the work organization must have the following structural characteristics:

1   There has to be a unified and objectifiable concept of performance against which in principle *all* the positions of the organizational status system can be assessed.
2   There have to be authorities who, firstly, are in a position to assess the performance value of everything that is done by all the participants in the work process and who, secondly, are able to ensure that no other criteria for the evaluation of an individual's status are considered relevant apart from the assessment of action in terms of performance.

Defining such a *concept of performance* runs into difficulties. The four functions listed above that are expected to follow from the realization of the achievement principle already contain two different concepts of performance. In functions 1 and 2 performance is considered in terms of the individual *outlay*—its subjective costs. However, in functions 3 and 4 performance is a question of the economic *yield* from work. Even if it were possible to construct a scale on which the value of the performance of every occupant of every position could be represented (and this is dubious given the extensive functional and hierarchical differentiation of economic organizations), this scale would be very different depending on whether it was constructed in terms of outlay or in terms of yield. The achievement principle itself thus contains an unexplicated dualism of two different criteria of performance. In particular the following dilemma results: if we decide that the yield criterion will be decisive, then we get into the logical and empirical difficulties which have led to the collapse of the theorem of marginal productivity. Alternatively, if we decide that the outlay criterion is the decisive one, then we can no longer compare with each other positions which, according to our previous assumptions, presuppose conformity with normative orientations rather than the incurring of material or non-material costs.

If we continue to argue in terms of explicating a functional model and for the moment avoid any reference to observable processes, then the question has to be posed as to the *assessing authority* which is meant to gauge 'performance' and thus ascribe status. According to the model, status distribution by performance involves not only particular characteristics of individuals' work behaviour, but, just as importantly, also the institutionalized possibility that this behaviour can be perceived and competently assessed by those authorities who control the distribution of organizational status attributes. The assessing authority therefore has to have a minimum of *competence* as precondition for the successful occurrence of the sequence: behaviour—assessment—status ascription/status legitimation. If we assume that this competence is not concentrated at one point, then we are implying that status assessment is horizontally and vertically decentralized. In fact for each case the immediate superior plays an important part in the assessment. Yet even if we accept the dubious idea that 'objective' observation (i.e. job analysis) of the relevant dimensions can yield a valid vertical classification of individuals and positions, this only leads to the further problem that in economic organizations the institutional processes of perception and assessment are in no way basically orientated to the allegedly objective criteria of performance.

The preceding discussion has clarified the normative model of the achievement principle and the achieving society, first of all with reference to the dependent variables—the dimensions of status which are meant to be determined by performance and by performance alone. In addition, we have described the functions through fulfilment of which this normative structure claims its validity; a society's status system can claim legitimacy to the extent that the conditions of the model are fulfilled in practice. We have seen that the concept of performance contains a certain inconsistency between the cost aspect and the output aspect. Further, we have established that to apply the achievement principle is to presuppose that the requirements of the different workroles of an organized system have a certain minimum similarity which enables them to be represented on a hierarchical continuum. This similarity must not simply exist objectively, but must also be competently and reliably perceived by the relevant authorities of the organizational system.

The subsequent course of this study follows from these analytical and classificatory preliminary considerations. Taking in turn each dimension of relative status within organizations—promotion, recruitment and income[4]—we will investigate whether, to what extent and to what degree of exclusivity a concept of performance can be considered as the variable which determines status. The answers will depend on whether the two necessary structural characteristics of the workplace are present or not. Further, the study will investigate the extent of the existence of additional and alternative determinants of status and, given such other mechanisms of status ascription, to what extent we can still talk of the fulfilment of those four functions from which the normative model of the achievement society derives its legitimating power.

Since this study is not an empirical investigation of one organization or of one organizational stratum, it will draw on empirical studies of different status groups within very different organizations (and these studies will be cited for purposes of discussion and demonstration, not as any final verification of the theses developed here). The aim of the study is to formulate hypotheses as to the trend in the development of the mechanisms of status distribution in industrial societies. This hypothesized trend should be considered as empirical to the extent that it can be used as a preliminary basis for empirical research.

[4] The following discussion only tangentially considers the formal authority dimension of status, since here it is clearest that mechanisms of domination intervene which are independent of performance.

3

Occupational recruitment and occupational mobility within organizations: the functions of the achievement principle

Sociological literature on stratification and mobility distinguishes between intergenerational mobility and intragenerational mobility.[1] The most important form of intragenerational mobility is vertical movement between different positions of an organization or within the institutionalized sectors of society. When this mobility takes the form of a vertical change of occupational positions and the change itself is based on an institutionalized sequence, then it is termed career or occupational mobility.[2]

Occupational mobility is meant to be governed by the achievement principle: if the individual is able to demonstrate a certain level of performance or contribution, measured according to a specific standard, then this is a necessary and sufficient condition for upward mobility.[3]

Occupational positions are graded hierarchically on several dimensions of status. Which dimensions apply to a particular position will vary according to organization and sector,[4] but the most important dimensions for all positions are normally considered to be income, prestige and formal authority, variously combined and weighted.

However, for the purposes of this critique of the achievement principle, the characteristics of status (which lie along the three listed dimensions) are less interesting than the preconditions for actually acquiring status. Precisely the claim of the achievement principle is that it introduces a 'rational' or 'just' method of organization, such that positions with varying amounts of honour or prestige can be ranked according to a single independent criterion. Starting from the changes in the nature of industrial work roles which we have hypothesized, this chapter will investigate two questions. Firstly, what characteristics of individuals or groups are empirically decisive for initiating the process of social mobility in

[1] For a typology of the different forms of social mobility, cf. T. Caplow, *The sociology of work* (Minneapolis 1954), 59ff.
[2] Cf. W. L. Slocum, *Occupational careers* (Chicago 1966).
[3] Downward mobility is partly subject to different rules and is not discussed here.
[4] For the problem of the different dimensions of status, cf. G. Lenski, *Power and privilege* (New York 1966).

formal organizations? Secondly, can these characteristics be subsumed under the category of functional importance, or do they belong rather to other elements of the work role?[5]

1   The functionalist theory of stratification: achievement as a criterion of status ascription in society

One of the most influential theories of social stratification, Davis and Moore's functionalist theory of stratification,[6] sanctifies at a macro-sociological level the achievement principle's claim to validity. The theory assumes that an individual's status is constituted both by his inborn talents, incarnating his ability to perform, and by the functional importance of his particular form of work for the maintenance of the social system. Davis and Moore base their model of status ascription in society as a whole on a sociologically expanded version of price theory: because of the basic *shortage* of talents, the *ability* to solve problems that are important for the society commands a high price (equal to high status) on the labour market. This price mechanism is also controlled by the criterion of functional importance, and this importance would have to be assessed by an authority encompassing the whole society.[7]

Positing such an authority which evaluates and defines the relative importance of the necessary performance value and then honours it accordingly has obvious ideological overtones. Tumin[8]

[5] This formulation of the problem is identical to one made 50 years ago by Schumpeter in a discussion of the theory of distribution in economics: 'It is . . . in practice often quite difficult to determine whether [in the case of individual movements in the labour market] these depend on occupational qualification (learning, habituation, individual adaptation to particular tasks), on social or national barriers as opposed to inborn characteristics, or indeed on what they depend. . . . This difficulty is especially noticeable in the case of the "vertical mobility" of labour power. Indeed, it is in no way clear what the difference is between the abilities required at one position and those at a position subordinate to it. Are the abilities qualitatively different? Are the "higher" abilities actually a "higher" form of the same abilities? Is there in fact any difference at all? All these abilities are ranked in some sort of scale, but how are they in reality related to each other? Which of them is inborn, acquired or simply activated by opportunity, or even exists at all? Further, it is unclear how the ability to acquire a position is related to the ability to fulfil it satisfactorily, and how the level of reward for performance is related to the level of performance itself as measured on another scale.' J. A. Schumpeter, 'Das Grundprinzip der Verteilungstheorie', *Arch. f. Soz. wiss. u. Soz. pol.* 42 (1916–17), 67–8.
[6] K. Davis and W. E. Moore, 'Some principles of stratification', in Bendix and Lipset, *Class, status and power*, 47–53.
[7] On the critique of functionalist stratification theory, see R. Mayntz, 'Kritische Bemerkungen zur funktionalistischen Schichtungstheorie', *KZfSS* 5 (1961), 10–28.
[8] M. M. Tumin, 'Some principles of stratification: a critical analysis', in Bendix and Lipset, *Class, status and power*, 53–9.

points out in a similar objection that the category of 'functional importance' has no empirical value, and in his reply Davis[9] has to make an implicit concession. He concretizes the concept of functional importance by citing examples which involve military, political or economic imperatives, yet in fact this concretization depends on assuming a situation where there is an explicit problem to be resolved, so that functional importance is defined by the interests which control the situation:

> Rough measures of functional importance are in fact applied in practice. In wartime, for example, decisions are made as to which industries and occupations will have priority in capital equipment, labor recruitment, raw materials, etc. In totalitarian countries the same is done in peacetime, as also in underdeveloped areas attempting to maximize their social and economic modernization. . . . There is nothing mystical about functional importance.[10]

However, outside of these extreme situations, the commonsense obviousness of the criterion of functional importance simply dissolves. The value of work in a particular occupation is claimed to result from its functional importance, yet—at least at a macrosociological level—this functional importance is the result of an arbitrary decision: functional importance therefore provides only a circular pseudo-proof of the connection between performance and status.[11]

Attempts to confirm empirically the functionalist theory of stratification[12] have up to now remained tied to the other determinant of status given by Davis and Moore. The idea of 'talent', obviously meant at first in a biological sense, is now expanded to include other dimensions of qualification such as 'acquired knowledge and ability', 'stress of work effort', etc. At the same time the dependent variable,

---

[9] K. Davis, 'Reply to Tumin', in Bendix and Lipset, *Class, status and power*, 59–62.

[10] *Ibid.*, 60.

[11] Davis and Moore are not alone in explaining social stratification in terms of the extent of the different functional qualifications and of the strains typically involved in the work role: such an explanation is accepted by many textbooks, theories and studies on social stratification. Cf., as typical of many, B. Barber, *Social stratification* (New York 1957), 24ff.: 'The greater the amount of knowledge or responsibility, or the two in combination, required for performance in a given role, the higher the stratificational position of that position. . . . Low positions in the systems of stratification in a society go to those individuals whose full time social roles require little knowledge and responsibility.' G. Lenski, *Power and privilege*, is within stratification theory one of the few positions which attempt to explain stratification through possession of power over the sources of surplus value, rather than through the content of occupational roles.

[12] Of the many such attempts, only two are discussed here: R. L. Simpson and I. H. Simpson, 'Correlates and estimation of occupational prestige', *AJS* 66 (1960), 135–40; and L. Kriesberg, 'The bases of occupational prestige: the case of dentists', *ASR* 27 (1962), 238–44.

the social rewards for job 'performance', is not tested to the extent that the theory demands: thus both Simpson and Simpson and also Kriesberg investigate the dependence of only one status dimension—that of prestige—on categories of performance ability.

Simpson and Simpson based their study on an occupational prestige scale derived from an NORC national survey. They presented the occupational definitions from the scale to a group of 21 students, who had to estimate the extent of 'skill' and 'responsibility' needed to carry out each occupation.[13] As expected, the resulting correlations between the rank order of the NORC scale and the students' judgements of the occupational roles were very high: prestige correlated with 'skill' with $r = 0.949$ and with 'responsibility' with $r = 0.933$.

However, two objections have to be made to this result and they make it as good as useless as a proof of the functionalist theory of stratification. (1) It is impossible to believe that on the basis of their everyday experience and without any methodologically controlled workplace observation etc., the respondents would have been in a position accurately to assess the 90 different jobs. In any case, the actual occupations given were frequently vaguely defined and needed to be further differentiated. (2) A correlation says nothing as to the direction of the causal relationship: this result could only be used as part of a proof of the functionalist stratification theory if it could be demonstrated that 'skill' and 'responsibility' *caused* prestige.

The first objection obviously strengthens the second, for it leads to the suspicion that when the students were assessing a job they could not have had in mind an occupation as actually carried out, for this must have been a reality beyond the horizon of their perception: instead their judgements must have been based on cultural definitions of the prestige value of each occupation. This mechanism is tantamount to a reversal of the causal relationship. However, the authors attempt to meet this argument by calculating the correlations separately for the individual occupational groups of the NORC catalogue, and this does result in significantly different correlation coefficients. They conclude that:

> The fact that substantially different patterns appeared in the different *situses* indicates that the rater's judgements did not simply reflect a halo from the occupations' general prestige.[14]

However, this additional calculation is in no way sufficient to establish a causal relationship of the sort the authors intend to. It

[13] The students were also asked to give estimates of 'autonomy', a category which however is irrelevant for the authors' intended test of Davis and Moore's theory.
[14] Simpson and Simpson, 'Correlates and estimation of occupational prestige', 138.

could certainly be the case that the assessment of the requirements
of the occupation was indeed not shaped by 'the occupations'
general prestige', but rather by the *specific* subcultural standards of
prestige which determined the *students'* perspectives.[15]

A methodologically more exact study[16] of the determinants of
occupational prestige (though limited to the assessment of only one
occupation, that of dentists) comes to conclusions which are incompatible with the functionalist stratification theory model. Kriesberg
first investigated three groups of factors to see whether they were
relevant for the original explanation of occupational prestige:
(1) 'scarcity' and 'importance' (corresponding to the factors assumed
by Davis and Moore), (2) 'valued attributes' such as 'money' and
'social origin' (these would correspond to an explanation of prestige
as being derived from another status attribute or from ascriptive
norms) and (3) the frequency and type of the estimators' own
individual experience of the performance of the groups being assessed (thus taking account of the intervening variable of 'cognitive
distance').

Kriesberg found that none of the three hypothetical determinants
of occupational prestige could explain the empirical prestige ranking which resulted from the respondents' individual assessment of
dentists. Even when all three factors were taken together they did
not result in a correlation with any explanatory power. Occupational prestige cannot therefore be explained in terms of the functional elements of the occupational role:

> So far we have been assuming that people have clear notions of the
> particular characteristics of an occupation and an articulated set of
> beliefs about these characteristics that are related to their attribution
> of prestige. Another kind of explanation must be considered. It may be
> that a person accords an occupation high prestige because he knows as
> a matter of fact that most persons accord members of that occupation
> high prestige.[17]

[15] One further attempt to prove the functionalist stratification theory
need not be discussed here, since it basically adds little new: J. Fromkin
and A. J. Jaffe, 'Occupational skill and socio-economic structure', *AJS* 59
(1953–4), 42–8.

In a report on studies of occupational prestige, A. F. Davies has warned
against a naive causal interpretation of empirical prestige hierarchies,
pointing out that (1) cultural and (2) cognitive factors intervene between
the evaluator and the evaluation itself: (1) 'Judgements of the prestige of
occupations will vary notably with the social status or social class position
of informants.' (2) In addition, the 'differences which people find in the
"nearer reaches" to themselves' are based on more reliable perception
and are subjectively more important to them. Thus, extra information
and status-specific preferences lead to a 'distortion' in the assessment of
prestige. A. F. Davies, 'Prestige of occupations', *BJS* 3 (1952), 134–7,
here 134–5.

[16] Kriesberg, 'The bases of occupational prestige'.

[17] *Ibid.*, 241.

According to this alternative explanation, prestige does not result from the fact that *the people who are being evaluated* fulfil particular functionally necessary qualifications of their occupational roles, but rather from the fact that the *people who evaluate them* have learnt and obey certain norms as to what the legitimate hierarchies of prestige actually are. Kriesberg's proposed explanation involves the assumption that the empirical pattern of prestige distribution depends more on knowledge of an institutionalized system of norms than on the perception of some or other elements of what is being assessed, namely the occupational role itself. The following test impressively confirms the importance of this 'second-hand experience' (Gehlen). The author establishes that 'the single variable, the respondent rating of the professional occupations compared to the non-professional occupations, seems more highly related to the prestige accorded dentists' than the observation of characteristics of the occupational role.[18]

Of the persons who assessed the prestige of 'professions' in relation to 'non-professions':	Percentage who rated the prestige of dentists as 'above average'
'a lot higher'	82
'a bit higher'	65
'a little higher'	49
'the same'	29
'less'	36

In the light of this result the (relatively weak) correlations between occupational role characteristics and prestige or status also have to be interpreted in a new way. It is in fact probable that not only are assessments of prestige determined by cultural norms of prestige (and not only by functional criteria of the occupational role), but so also is the assessment of the characteristics of the occupational role itself. If this were not the case, then cognitive dissonance would emerge between norms and observation. Although the dentist's role may still have a relatively high social visibility, and as a result the adjustment of observation to normative standards of prestige has to override a remnant of direct experience, Kriesberg gains the impression that: 'It is possible that a person's evaluation of the social importance of an occupation may be modified ... so that it is made consistent with the prestige hierarchy as he learned it.'[19] In this case:

[18] *Ibid.*, 242.
[19] *Ibid.*

perceived occupational prestige would have more effect upon perceptions of at least some other occupational characteristics than vice versa. ... Persons may well have a clearer and more definite perception of the prestige hierarchy than the income, skill, social importance and other occupational hierarchies. People have many more cues ... about the relative prestige shown members of different occupations than about the relative standing of occupations according to other criteria.[20]

It is obvious how important this result is for explaining how social status is ascribed: if what Kriesberg has shown for the dentist's occupational role is the general case (and the dentist's role is in no relevant way an extreme case), then the distribution of status attributes could not be explained through the functions of the occupational role, as the achieving society model would have it. Instead, the distribution of status would have to be explained by the existence of a dominant normative hierarchy of values, which is oriented to the symbolic connotations of occupational roles, and which ranks roles in higher or lower positions quite independently of their functional content.

Kriesberg's study and the conclusions which follow from it deny Davis and Moore's proposed theory of social stratification its explanatory power: neither the (operationally contentless) criterion of 'functional importance' nor the measure of 'talent' can tackle the problem of how status attributes are distributed.

However, this result cannot be directly applied to the processes of status ascription inside organizations, i.e. to the micro-sociological level. There are two differences which have to be considered between the macro-sociological level with which Davis and Moore were concerned and the micro-sociological level. What for total social systems is the exception, is for formal (i.e. goal-oriented) organizations the rule. In other words, only in extreme cases, such as in a war threatening the existence of the whole society, does the overall social system have an explicit aim, yet in formal organizations it is the existence of such an explicit aim which provides a firm reference point for the application of the criterion of 'functional importance'.[21] In addition, one could assume that the *functional* characteristics of the occupational role are central in the ascription of status inside an organization and in occupational mobility, so that therefore, unlike status distribution at the macro-level, status at this micro-level does not depend very much on *normative* models of society. Nonetheless, the remainder of this chapter will show that other factors mean that this assumption has to be severely restricted.

[20] *Ibid.*, 243.
[21] This applies at least for organizations which have a one-dimensional goal function. Cf. A. Etzioni, 'Industrial sociology: the study of economic organizations', in Etzioni (ed.), *Complex organizations* (New York 1964), 130–42.

2   Occupational role identity: central or peripheral element of the occupational role?

In formal organizations, if social mobility is based on the achievement principle, then its typical form is *promotion*[22] on the basis of proved performance or merit defined with reference to the organization's objective. According to this model, the decisive factor for the allocation of prestige, authority or income status is assessments of performance made by higher authorities in the organization whose position legitimizes them to distribute status to those below them. In the liberal academic occupations (the professions), we also encounter another form of performance assessment, namely assessment by the subordinate participants in the cooperative relationship: thus politicians' influence is increased by the acclamation of electors and party members, the professional career of doctors and lawyers is promoted by their clients' satisfaction.

In both cases, whether performance can be decisive for the occupational mobility process depends upon two conditions which we have already seen in a general form in our previous analysis of the achievement principle:

1   The concept of performance must have operational content in the given situation: the character of the technological working conditions must objectively allow a positive contribution to the oragnization's aim to be identified as such, and also to be ascribed to the work of a *particular person*. Our hypothesis here is that on technological grounds, namely everywhere where 'initiatory' influence is replaced by 'preventive' influence, the category of performance cannot any longer be positively ascribed to individuals. Instead, performance can only be understood negatively, as 'preventive' or 'avoidance' behaviour. Because of its normative (and non-technical) structure, this behaviour no longer takes the form of individual ability, but rather merely of the *collective* following of normative orientations.

2   The second functional condition for the effectiveness of the achievement principle is the organizationally-produced *possibility* that, in the positions where technological change has not yet replaced 'individual-positive' performance with merely 'collective-negative functioning', superiors and subordinates will also actually recognize and competently assess those manifestations of individual performance which do occur. This possibility is organizationally mediated: a competent assessment of 'performance' is only possible by a person in authority if he has similar knowledge and experience to the person whom he is assessing, and if he also is only separated

[22] Cf. S. M. Lipset and R. Bendix, 'Social mobility and occupational career patterns', *AJS* 57 (1952), 366–74, 494–504; Fürstenberg, *Probleme der Lohnstruktur*.

from what he is assessing by a small perceptual distance. As for this second condition, our hypothesis also follows from the discussion in the introductory chapter. Within the hierarchy of a formal organization, a discontinuous qualification structure, together with the physical, optical and acoustic relaxation of the supervisory relationship (especially for directly productive labour), creates organizational obstacles to a competent assessment of performance, even where technological changes have not yet made work lose its character of 'individually productive' activity.[23]

The first of these conditions, then, is the *technological character-istics* of work: are these such that the worker's activity results in a product which is ascribable to a particular individual and which *objectifies* his capacity for work? The second condition is the organizational structure within which the work occurs: if the technical preconditions for an 'objectification of the product' do exist, does the organizational framework of work allow the individual to *demonstrate* his capacity for work *to* the relevant authorities (relevant that is, for his promotion)? The corresponding hypotheses answer both these questions in the negative. If these hypotheses prove to be valid, then workers' self-understanding must encounter problems which we can conceptualize as a threatening of occupational identity.

However, both these hypotheses should not yet be tested against the empirical material which can be used for secondary analysis. This will only be possible when we have drawn some conclusions from the assumptions and hypotheses which have been formulated up to this stage in the study.

Our basic assumption is that the achievement principle is a pre-scriptive model of status distribution, providing for formal organizations in industrial societies the sole principle by which social status is legitimated, where status includes both differences in existing status and changes of status by means of occupational mobility.

Both the hypotheses consider interconnected technical and organizational structural changes in formal work organizations as independent variables. It is assumed, first, that technological changes modify the character of work in such a way that they render largely

[23] The loss of the chance socially to demonstrate occupational identity does not only result in the relevant reference groups being unable to understand clearly or to judge competently the specialized work processes involved. Merton, following Roethlisberger, describes a still more drastic form of 'social invisibility': 'The growing subdivision of work tasks creates numberless new occupations for which, as Roethlisberger has observed, there exist no occupational names that have any social significance outside of the particular industry, factory or department in many cases. The splintering of work tasks involves loss of public identity of the job.' R. K. Merton, 'The machine, the worker and the engineer', in S. Nosow and W. H. Form (eds.), *Man, work and society* (New York 1962), 82–7, here 83.

obsolete that type of work which is 'production' based on individual *ability*: secondly, that organizational changes restrict the *social perception* of the individual's work capacity and thus remove the preconditions for any evaluation of performance which is based strictly on the aims of the organization (and an evaluation is for us 'rational' to the extent that it is in terms of the organization's aims). Both at the level of occupational behaviour of individuals and at the level of organizational mechanisms of status distribution, this should entail the following consequences.

In many cases technological working conditions necessitate primarily the relatively passive and sensitive operation of machinery and obedience to regulatory norms, so that productivity cannot any longer be ascribed to specific individuals. Other types of performance certainly are still subjectively experienced and understood in terms of the model of 'producing', yet because of organizational changes it is no longer possible socially to demonstrate them as such: they cannot therefore any longer be used in any intelligible justification of claims for social status. When both these changes occur together, then they create a conflict with the still firmly institutionalized principle that status is legitimated by performance. Given the ideologically-maintained fiction that there is a functionally necessary link betwen status and performance, both the technological restriction of productive work ascribable to specific individuals and equally the organizational limits on the supervision of performance create a legitimacy vacuum.

This vacuum is filled partly by *performance substitutes,* such as occupational symbols and ideologies. These are not tied to the technological and perceptual limits of the workplace and they can thus help to overcome the work-role identity crisis. For example, the workers' consciousness is no longer based on the ability to produce and on the chance to demonstrate this ability, for this chance is limited by the conditions of technical and automated work. Instead, workers understand their situation through extra-functional orientations (that is, orientations which are completely external to the work role itself and its rational requirements), acquired in extensive career and pre-career socialization processes.

If the changes we have analysed are significant ones, then we would expect them to lead to changes too at the other end of the authority relationships in work. We would expect that if the individual labour ability used in production and administrative organizations is 'socially invisible', then this leaves the authorities who judge performance with no alternative but to judge the individual's performance capacity symbolically, in other words, to use indicators of performance which more and more diverge from the core of task-adequate performance. One could take as examples of such indicators symbols of performance which are acquired externally to the organization, institutional loyalties, criteria of origin and other ascriptive criteria or extrafunctional attributes. Without exception, these are criteria which are only loosely (if at all) connected with the productive aims of the organization, but which serve instead to stabilize relationships of economic and cultural domination.

Since individuals remain forced to acquire differential status in terms of their individual performance ability, and since equally organizations have to explain differential status in these same terms, both individual strategies of social mobility and organizational criteria for promotion are based on the category of extrafunctional orientations and symbols.

This functional connection is remarkable for its paradoxical character. The achievement principle has a rigid authority, for it claims to be the sole determination of the system of status distribution within organizations. In the work conditions discussed above, this, together with the principle's subjective correlate of an individualistic orientation to social mobility, itself leads to irrational indicators and symbols of work having to be used and taken as 'performance', so that therefore these indicators themselves acquire an important function within the process of organizational status distribution and status change.

Berger and Luckmann[24] have analysed the conflict-laden consequences for personal identity which stem from an individualistic orientation to social mobility. However, their discussion is within a frame of reference which merely takes account of the macro-sociological development tendencies of industrial societies, of which the most important elements are the decline of class consciousness, the extension of mobility orientation, status inconsistency and the segmentalization of institutional sectors. Arguments of the organizational sociology type only occur at the margin of their discussion:

> Performances in the hierarchical institutional bureaucracies, for example, minimize status uncertainty within that sphere. Yet we may assert with confidence that in modern life individuals are not unequivocally perceived in a status hierarchy by others and, in consequence, by themselves.[25]

This touches on our concern with the blocked chances of demonstrating ocupational identity: however, occupational identity is not first threatened *between* the institutional sectors, but rather, as our previous discussion has shown, already occurs within the 'hierarchical institutional bureaucracies' themselves.

There is no reason why the behavioural consequences of this 'underdefinition of identity' should consist exclusively, as the authors seems to assume, in the attempt to reconstruct outside the work role

---

[24] T. Luckmann and P. Berger, 'Social mobility and personal identity', *Eur. Arch. f. Soz.* 5 (1964), 331–44.
[25] *Ibid.*, 334.

the self-definition which has become impossible within it. Although there is in fact much evidence of this form of compensation, the continuing influence of the work role on other role sectors, together with some aspects of the professionalization thesis, suggests that the lost chances of identity can also to a certain extent be regained through stressing 'peripheral' elements of the *occupational* role. To say this is not to deny the importance of privatized substitutes in the consumption sphere for the lost occupational identity. However, precisely if one, like Berger and Luckmann, sees status conscious-ness and upward mobility orientation as quasi-religious cultural imperatives, and if one also posits a reduction of mobility which is linked to 'central' role elements and therefore dependent on per-formance, it appears plausible to assume that the mechanism which both strengthens personal identity and promotes social mobility is extrafunctional forms of identification with the occupational role. In this way orientation to social mobility[26] could on the one hand be seen as one cause of the threat to identity (this is Berger and Luckmann's argument) and *at the same time* it could be interpreted as the functional reference point through which the threat to identity is compensated for. It is implausible that privatistic type compensatory mechanisms (located in the spheres of criminality, 'leisure', religion, sex, etc.) could *by themselves* restore identity dam-aged in the occupational role, for these mechanisms are institution-ally isolated from the work sector and cannot be perceived by the authorities who are relevant for promotion. It follows that these compensatory mechanisms are in fact partly inconsistent with the assumed mobility orientation, for this remains, as before, realized through work in an occupation. This argument too leads us to expect that the existing mobility orientation will coexist with the attempt to stabilize the precarious occupational role identity with the help of extrafunctional elements of the *occupational role itself*.[27]

[26] In America, as elsewhere, there are clear social structural limits on the extent to which this mobility orientation has spread through the society: cf. B. C. Rosen, 'The achievement syndrome: a psychocultural dimension of social stratification', *ASR* 21 (1956), 203–11; H. Hyman, 'The value system of different classes', in Bendix and Lipset, *Class, status and power* (1st edn, New York 1953), 426–42; H. Crockett, 'The achievement motive and differential mobility in the United States', *ASR* 27 (1962), 191–204.

[27] Bensman and Rosenberg give an impressionistic description of the extent and breadth of the role elements which are crystallized by the secondary socialization processes in bureaucratic work organizations: 'Old habits are discarded and new habits are nurtured. The would-be success learns when to simulate enthusiasm, compassion, interest, concern, modesty, confidence, and mastery; when to smile, with whom to laugh and how intimate and friendly he can be with other people. He selects his home and his residential area with care; he buys his clothes and chooses styles with an eye to their probable reception in his office. He reads or pretends to have read the right books, the right magazines, and the right newspapers. All this will be reflected in the "right line of conversation" which he adapts

With this thesis we reach the stage at which we can draw upon empirical material to illustrate and confirm the argument. The material used covers widely varying levels within very different organizations, and this not just for pragmatic research reasons. Using a relatively unspecific set of empirical studies for secondary analysis is also justified if we remember that the phenomena we have assumed to exist should occur at all levels and within all sectors of occupational work in industrial and bureaucratic organizations: their existence therefore has to be proved by using the most heterogenous material possible. In the analysis of the empirical material we will also retain the distinction already introduced above between (1) subjective compensations for the threat to occupational role identity and (2) extrafunctional organizational criteria for evaluation and promotion.

We have assumed a growth in the importance of extrafunctional determinants of status, and this is based on an analytical distinction which can be seen to have been used in sociology since Max Weber's analysis of bureaucracy. Following Weber, R. M. Marsh[28] defines the difference between 'bureaucratic' and 'extrabureaucratic' determinants of promotion as follows:

> *Bureaucratic* determinants of advancement [are]: 1. achievement, 2. seniority . . . all determinants of advancement other than seniority and achievement will be referred to as *extrabureaucratic* determinants: 1. the purchase of substantive posts by officials, 2. family background, 3. age of officials, 4. method of recruitment to the bureaucracy, whenever this entails special favors, preferential treatment instead of the universal application of achievement norms.[29]

This distinction between impersonal, achievement-oriented and bureaucratic selection mechanisms in organizations and personal, non-achievement-oriented, 'extrabureaucratic' ones is paralleled at the subjective level by a classification of the different role elements. At the level of the work role Dahrendorf[30] therefore distinguishes between functional and extrafunctional skills. Skills are functional if they are 'developed with reference to the technological requirements of given work processes,'[31] while extrafunctional skills are:

> not primarily related to the purely technical claims of the work process, but far more to its organizational and social context. They designate

---

as his own. . . . He joins the right party and espouses the political ideology of his fellows.' J. Bensman and B. Rosenberg, 'The meaning of work in bureaucratic society', in M. Stein *et al.* (eds.), *Identity and anxiety* (New York 1960), 183–4.

[28] R. M. Marsh, 'Formal organization and promotion in a pre-industrial society', *ASR* 26 (1961), 547–56.

[29] *Ibid.*, 548.

[30] R. Dahrendorf, 'Industrielle Fertigkeiten und soziale Schichtung'.

[31] *Ibid.*, 549.

decisions of their carriers ... therefore strictly speaking they are not absolutely necessary for the process of production.[32]

Following G. Incheiser,[33] H. P. Dreitzel[34] makes a similar distinction between *ability to perform* and *ability to succeed*. Finally, for the same situation Weinstock distinguishes between central and peripheral role elements:

> The central role elements consist of the strictly occupational requirements. The term 'central', in the case of the teacher, covers the instrumental or performance aspects of the role, such as technical knowledge and educational requirements. The peripheral elements may be distinguished by their reference to the non-technical, institutionally required social aspects of the role.[35]

Using this analytical distinction we can now formulate the two empirical questions which the subsequent sections of this study will investigate:

1   Is only performance-related knowledge and ability ('bureaucratic', 'functional' or 'central' role elements) accumulated before or during upward mobility within organizations? Alternatively, to what extent can it be shown that, in addition to this, mobility also entails the acquisition of extrafunctional symbols and ideologies?
2   Do the authorities responsible for mobility within organizations promote and evaluate according to measures of functional performance? Alternatively, are the authorities oriented to extrafunctional and ascriptive criteria for promotion?

If in both cases we find indications that the second alternative occurs, then the general hypothesis will be taken as confirmed.

3   Mobility orientation and peripheral elements of occupational role identity

The introductory chapter pointed out how important regulatory norms and 'avoidance rules' are if technical and bureaucratic work roles are to function smoothly. These rules form part of a more or less general work ethic, which has to be concretized for each particular workplace. It is thus an oversimplification to see regulatory norms as not being 'central' or 'functional' elements of the occupational role. Instead, if we consider the elements of the work role as lying on a continuum, then these rules must fall on the borderline between the functional and the extrafunctional areas.

[32] *Ibid.*, 554.
[33] G. Inchheiser, *Kritik des Erfolges* (Leipzig 1930).
[34] H. P. Dreitzel, *Elitebegriff und Sozialstruktur* (Stuttgart 1962).
[35] A. Weinstock, 'Role elements: a link between acculturation and occupational status', *BJS* 14 (1963), 144–9, here 145.

In his analysis of bureaucratic roles R. K. Merton[36] has shown how such originally functional orientations can lose their instrumental connection to the workplace: as they become ritualized they become the basis of a social personality which becomes independent of the work and performance context. Such a ritualistic stylization of bureaucratic virtues develops even despite its partial dysfunctionality. Normative sentiments

> are often more intense than is technically necessary.... This very emphasis leads to a transference of the sentiments from the aims of the organization on to the particular details of behavior required by the rules.... This emphasis ... develops into rigidities and an inability to adjust readily.... Thus, the very elements which conduce toward efficiency in general produce inefficiency in specific instances.

For Merton it seems, norms thus become rigid and thereby dysfunctional through an inevitable process of objectification. However, this process only becomes comprehensible when it is analysed in terms of its very functionality, not for the organization's aims but rather for the status affirmation and occupational identity of the individual bureaucrat. Looked at from this perspective, the ossification of bureaucratic attitudes appears not so much a residue of occupational socialization processes, but primarily a means whereby, through the routine of applying rules impersonally, personal peculiarities can nonetheless be developed and demonstrated without formally breaking the ruling norms of the organization. When it becomes impossible to exercise 'initiatory' influence on the work result, or when at least this cannot be clearly observed by the authorities who matter for promotion, then ritualistic and tendentially even dysfunctional overfulfilment of norms can replace categories of occupational achievement and productivity. According to this interpretation, then, ritualism is not just a simple disturbance of the functioning of the organization, it is also a method of individual mobility in organizations. In this situation, a set of demonstrated virtues has become independent of the concrete work tasks and their instrumental solutions, and the bureaucrat is only too willing to see them as the benchmark against which his chances of social renumeration and social mobility are measured.

Several studies have shown that extrafunctional attitudes relevant for promotion are acquired in occupational training and in the initial period of occupational work, rather than through the objectification of occupational role elements. In their study, 'Elements of identification with an occupation', Becker and Carper[37] found that in the case of the professions the university plays a decisive part in

[36] R. K. Merton, 'Bureaucratic structure and personality', *Soc. Forc.* 17 (1940), 560–68.
[37] H. S. Becker and J. Carper, 'The elements of identification with an occupation', *ASR* 21 (1956), 341–8.

the occupational socialization process—they talk of the 'central character of graduate school in developing professional identifications'.[38] According to them, this socialization process at the university extends over four areas of the occupational role, and all of these apart from the second one must be considered as extrafunctional elements:

1 occupational signs and occupational ideology
2 commitment to task
3 loyalty to an organization
4 occupational status claims

In general 'these elements of identification affect the relative ease of an individual's mobility through occupational institutions', although not all the sets of attitudes acquired at university affect this social mobility in the same way. The set of attitudes summarized by 'commitment to task' involves a purely technical and functional achievement orientation fixated on a particular task or problem, yet this orientation can have results which actually restrict mobility. This occurs because, in organizations with a differentiated division of labour, if individuals follow their technical interests and apply themselves to a particular area, investing their occupational motivation in it, they are constrained to accumulate specialized productive knowledge and ability which cannot be simply transferred to other occupational positions (possibly granting such a person the reputation of being an expert is a way of compensating him for his blocked chances of mobility). This situation is frequent in organizations with a discontinuous qualification structure;[39] it shows that in such organizations, to possess rational productive knowledge and nothing else is not only no help to an occupational career, but can actually be a hindrance. This state of affairs is what Becker and Carper have in mind when they write:

> If, in identifying himself occupationally, an individual exhibits an intense identification with a particular institutional position or a particular set of tasks or with both of these, movement to some other position, or movement which involves a shift in the actual job done, becomes more difficult. The physiologists exemplify this tendency. Tied to their particular research problems and techniques, they are unable to envision themselves occupying any but the few positions they know of in which they can pursue these problems in the way they know best.[40]

Thus there is a conflict between the two sides of the occupational socialization process: between technical elements, which are instrumentally related to the occupational tasks, and extrafunctional ones,

[38] *Ibid.*, 341.
[39] Cf. P. M. Blau, *Exchange and power in social life* (New York 1964), 161–7.
[40] Becker and Carper, 'The elements of identification with an occupation', 348.

which are oriented to the organization's status quo and to the value systems that dominate it. The conflict seems always to be resolved in favour of the extrafunctional elements because (a) the individual is committed to individual social mobility and (b) the organization assesses him as an individual. The domination of the extrafunctional elements means that there is an acceptance of the relationships of domination within the institution which control access to the desired occupational positions. M. Seeman and J. W. Evans[41] have followed this process in a longitudinal study investigating attitudinal change in young doctors during their internship (the period at the end of which it is decided whether or not the young doctor will be given a permanent post in a hospital). The authors administered a questionnaire to interns at the beginning and end of their internship, eliciting from them authoritarian and egalitarian attitudes towards their two most important reference groups, the nurses and the doctors. The aim was to show the interns' status consciousness (i.e. their claims to prestige and authority, together with their social distance from their two reference groups) during the occupational socialization process.

The results clearly confirm the acquisition of nonfunctional role elements:

> We believe the data support the conclusion that the year of apprenticeship has, indeed, made the interns more status minded. At the end of the year they appear to see themselves as more nearly equals of the other physicians, and in that degree their responses show increasing egalitarianism and in-group membership; but it is an equality which stresses the distance between this medical in-group and the out-group of lower-status-personnel.[42]

As in Merton's analysis of the bureaucratic role, here too there occurs an over-identification with the norms specific to the organization. However, in the case of the doctors' status consciousness it is very dubious whether this over-identification can be considered as a functional element of the occupational role:

> A comparison of the interns' status-attitudes at the close of the internship with the attitudes of the residents reveals what may be called a process of 'over-identification' upward. . . . Indeed, the interns typically change in a fashion that carries them ideologically away from the status views of the residents: they are more different from the residents at the end of the internship than at the beginning of the year.[43]

[41] M. Seeman and J. W. Evans, 'Apprenticeship and attitude change', *AJS* 67 (1961), 365–78.

[42] *Ibid.*, 372. Another study of doctors also shows this process clearly: L. V. Beale and L. Kriesberg, 'Career-relevant values of medical students', *J. Am. Med. Assoc.* 171 (1959), 1447–8. Medical students 'become more concerned with matters extrinsic to medical practice as they move through their medical school training.'

[43] Seeman and Evans, 'Apprenticeship and attitude change', 374.

Thus, while the official aim of the internship period is to equip the young doctor with practical medical knowledge and attitudes, in fact an important function of this period of medical training is to develop in the interns an occupational identity. This identity is composed of extrafunctional role elements and can therefore, unlike functional performance ability, be visibly demonstrated to everybody (i.e. to colleagues, nurses and patients) and then utilized symbolically to achieve occupational mobility.

The extrafunctional and subjective determinants of career mobility are also investigated in a study which attempts to explain the differing 'career success' of groups of people with the same social background. Coates and Pellegrin[44] wanted to answer the question 'why some individuals achieve more vertical mobility and career success than others in the same or similar occupational environments.'[45] They contrasted two groups of upper and lower management, and used qualitative interviews to locate the genesis and content of the managers' occupational role identity. The results were striking in that upper and lower management *agreed* as to the causes of their respective relative success or failure: neither group gave an explanation couched in terms of 'more' or 'less' quantitative achievement or ability. Instead, they explained their occupational fate in terms of differing normative orientations. From this result the authors consider themselves justified in rejecting the traditional theory of individual causality of occupational mobility, which 'centers in the traditional belief that career progress results from native ability and a variety of other individual attributes, hard work, and the demonstration of merit'.[46] They propose instead a situational explanation of career success, assuming the cause of relative mobility to be the definition of the situation which operated when occupational mobility began. This definition of the situation is mediated by the individual's cultural background, his college education and those significant others and their occupational aspirations whom the individual encountered at his *first* workplace. Along the lines of Merton's 'self-fulfilling prophecy', the authors find that it is the occupational identity constituted within the frame of reference of the role system specific to that particular first workplace which is decisive for subsequent successful mobility.

> Occupational placement and early career experiences lead individuals to adopt attitudes, values and behavior patterns which function as

[44] C. H. Coates and R. J. Pellegrin, 'Executives and supervisors: contrasting self-conceptions and conceptions of each other', in B. H. Stoodley (ed.), *Society and self* (New York, 1962), 48ff.; *idem*, 'Executives and supervisors: a situational theory of differential occupational mobility', *Soc. Forc.* 35 (1956), 121–6.
[45] Coates and Pellegrin, 'Executives and supervisors: contrasting self-conceptions . . .', 48.
[46] *Ibid.*, 121.

important positive or negative influences in subsequent career progress and occupational mobility.[47]

It is possible to interpret in the same way one of the findings of Lipset and Malm's Oakland mobility studies.[48] Their analysis of occupational destiny and patterns of upward mobility establishes that *initial* occupational position is very important for the process of occupational mobility:

> The first job that a man secures is about twice as important as his educational attainment in determining whether he ultimately winds up on the manual or on the non-manual side of the occupational scale, and about four times as important a determinant as his father's occupation.[49]

This fact is important for two reasons. Firstly, it confirms Coates and Pellegrin's thesis that the definition of the situation established at entrance to the occupational world is decisive for upward mobility, quite independent of the individual's performance ability. Secondly, it underlines that these determinants of success are largely independent of functional criteria: the individual's entrance to an occupational position proves to be very important for his subsequent occupational mobility, even though one would assume that this stage in his career would be the most difficult one in which to judge his functional performance.

The studies discussed so far all show that extrafunctional identities develop in the different sectors and the different status groups of industrial-bureaucratic occupational work. From a technical point of view these elements of the work role are 'peripheral', but they have the function of constituting an occupational role identity that is clear and visible to all relevant reference groups. The main component of the work role can no longer be the 'central' role elements, for in many cases work is a passive routine, making only limited demands on the worker; at the same time organizational obstacles to the observation of work by superiors make both the work process and those requirements it places on the worker socially invisible. For these reasons we have interpreted here extrafunctional identities as substitutes and symbols for performance, performance itself having now become abstract and intangible. The pressure towards this substitution comes from the rigidity with which the achievement principle links legitimate status claims to individual ability. The structural dilemma, the need to symbolize 'ability' by conformity, has the social function of pushing the mobility-oriented individual to accept the dominant normative patterns, on the

---

[47] *Ibid.*, 125. On the preceding discussion, cf. also Coates and Pellegrin, 'Executives and supervisors: informal factors in differential bureaucratic promotion', *Adm. Sc. Quart.* 2 (1957–8), 200–215.
[48] S. M. Lipset and F. T. Malm, 'First jobs and career patterns', *Am. J. Econ. and Soc.* 14 (1955), 247–61.
[49] *Ibid.*, 256.

stability of which the existence of the contemporary form of work and domination depends.

All the empirical knowledge which sociology has accumulated would lead us to expect that extrafunctional identities will not predominate to the same extent within all occupational status groups. From our hypothesis we can deduce three subsidiary hypotheses as to the distribution of extrafunctional identities.

1   In the lower class, unlike the middle class, the achievement principle is not important in primary socialization.[50] There exists here to a certain extent a dichotomous image of society,[51] while collective mobility is more important than improvements in individual status[52] and blocked chances of mobility are a frequent experience.[53] In general, therefore, we would expect less of an orientation to social mobility here than in the middle class. However, we have taken the desire for social mobility to be the driving force of the process whereby symbolic and ideological role elements are used to establish demonstrable occupational role identities. We can therefore assume that in the lower class occupational self-conception contains a lower proportion of peripheral role elements.

2   We argued that the pressure to symbolize performance by institutional loyalty results from, first, the organizationally-determined reduced chance that the result of a cooperatively-organized work process will be understood as objectifying the individual's ability to work. We can assume that these two conditions become more acute as we move from work with *things* through work with *symbols* to work with *people*. The order of these three types of work designates firstly a certain developmental trend in the frequency of the different forms of industrial work.[54] Secondly, from a 'vertical' perspective it also roughly designates the forms of work in organizational hierarchies: typically in industrial production, work with raw materials and products is allocated to the lowest status group, the middle status group of clerical workers is occupied with routine bureaucratic tasks, while management has the task of exercising authority, cooperating with reference groups external to the organization through personal negotiation, etc.

3   If this rough typology has any predictive value, it would mean that the level of 'objectifiability' of individual performance decreases as the scale is ascended. The need for a tangible self-definition and a socially visible demonstration of occupational

[50] Cf. Rosen, 'The achievement syndrome'.
[51] Cf. H. Popitz et al., *Das Gesellschaftsbild des Arbeiters* (Tübingen 1957).
[52] Cf. for example B. C. Stone, 'Mobility factors as they affect workers' attitudes and conduct towards incentive systems', *ASR* 17 (1952), 58–64.
[53] Cf. Lipset and Bendix, 'Social mobility and occupational career patterns'; E. Chinoy, 'The tradition of opportunity and the aspirations of automobile workers', *AJS* 57 (1952), 453–9.
[4] On this assumption cf. for example Slocum, *Occupational careers*, 26.

identity would be correspondingly greater in the upper areas of hierarchical organizations. At these levels status also needs more symbolic legitimation because the positions entail access to other high social rewards and to power resources.

We have thus named three groups of factors which lead us to expect that extrafunctional elements will make up a larger proportion of occupational role identity in the higher strata of organizations. To list them once again in summary form:

1   The cultural background of the middle class is more oriented to social mobility.
2   In work with symbols and with people (the dominant forms of work in the higher strata within organizations) qualification in central role elements is less 'socially visible'.
3   Positions with high social rewards and involving control of power resources need more legitimacy.

A study by Schein and Ott[55] confirms the expected high proportion of extrafunctional elements in occupational roles where all three groups of factors coincide. The study was designed to discover the extent and social distribution of Whyte's 'conformist social ethic' or Reismann's 'other directedness'. The authors took a stratified sample of 812 people, students, managers and workers, and questioned them on their attitudes to which areas of behaviour they considered their work role could legitimately control. Fifty items represented the different areas of behaviour, and for each item each respondent had to decide whether or not he considered that the employer or work organization could legitimately exert influence on it.

The areas of behaviour were so defined that they made up a scale of work-near ('job related') to work-distant ('highly personal'), areas; the construction of the scale was based on considering the elements of the work role as forming a continuum from central to peripheral ones. All the respondents agreed as to the ranking of the elements: they were less prepared to allow influence on the peripheral role elements than on the central ones:

> High legitimacy items all concern behavior at the work place and the company. The low legitimacy items concern family relationships, matters of taste in non-job related areas, place of residence, political and religious views and the like.[56]

However, this consensus amongst the respondents only confirms that the scale itself is valid: there are important differences between the individual subsamples. In fact, the readiness to accept organiza-

[55] E. H. Schein and J. S. Ott, 'The legitimacy of organizational influence', *AJS* 67 (1961), 681–9.
[56] *Ibid.*, 684.

tionally specific norms and interests as part of the definition of
one's own occupational role increases from workers up to managers,
with the differences between workers and students and managers
and students being significant at the p=0·001 level.

> There is a consistent and significant rise in the individual indexes with
> increasing proximity to the managerial role, reflecting an increasing
> willingness to regard more areas as legitimate areas of influence. . . . On
> most items there is a consistent rise in the index from labor to students
> to managers, reflecting the greater tendency of the managerial group
> to sanction influence. The largest differences occur between the labor
> and the management group, primarily in reference to attitude areas
> reflecting loyalty to the company, the subordinate's presentation of him-
> self during the working day, degree of autonomy from the company,
> personal morality, and some specific items like attitudes to unions. . . .
> For example 55 per cent of the managers . . . stated that it was legitimate
> to influence a subordinate's participation in non-company public activities,
> while only 10 per cent of the labor group agreed that it was legitimate.[57]

These results clearly show how strongly the norms and interests
of work organizations are linked to areas of life and behaviour
which have nothing to do with the functional needs of work, while
it is clear that the connection is stronger in the higher organizational strata: obviously, the stability of an organizational structure
of domination is strengthened by tight control over as many areas
of behaviour as possible of precisely its upper strata. However, at
the present stage of the argument the nature of this loyalty to an
organizational system of norms and domination is still unclear.
Loyalty could simply be the residue of occupational socialization
processes, or it could alternatively, as our hypothesis assumes, be
the symbolic substitute for the lost chances of effectively demonstrating achievement, a substitute which the individual utilizes
strategically to become upwardly mobile in his occupation.

A study by Stone[58] helps to clarify this question. Stone takes
social mobility in work organizations to be decisively determined
by (1) objective mobility chances (2) subjective motivation to mobility (3) loyalty to superiors relevant for promotion. He hypothesizes
that the causal relationships between these determinants are: (1)
factual upward mobility increases loyalty to the organization's
interests (2) factual mobility strengthens orientation to mobility
(3) mobility orientation likewise increases loyalty to the employer's
interests. From this point of view, the different normative orientations of manual and whitecollar workers can be explained by the
fact that typically the two status groups have different chances of
occupational mobility.

However, this argument is open to a simple objection. It is a

[57] *Ibid.*, 687, 689.
[58] Stone, 'Mobility factors . . .'.

well-documented sociological finding that the objective mobility chances of whitecollar workers and manual workers are not as different as the subjective aspirations of whitecollar consciousness wish to believe:[59] there are in fact strong tendencies in the direction of equal mobility chances for both status groups. The different normative orientations of the two status groups cannot therefore be explained by the 'learning effect' of factually-observed social change, but rather they have to be explained by the two groups' different cultural value systems as acquired in primary socialization. The specific mobility aspirations of the middle class then make up an independent determinant of the readiness of whitecollar workers to identify with their occupation, whether in the administrative or the commercial sector, and this is a determinant that Stone's model neglects. If we accept that this cultural factor operates independently, then we can expect not only that loyalty to the imposed organizational interests is independent of the factual chances of mobility, but also that it becomes effective precisely when practical experience no longer provides the certainty that real mobility chances do exist. Specifically, if institutionalized career paths shrink to a narrow hierarchical span (which in turn could be explained by the phenomena of external recruitment and discontinuous qualification structures), then the 'action parameter' which the whitecollar worker can manipulate to create the lucky accident of a dramatic jump in his career becomes not the central, but rather the peripheral elements of his role.

Such an interpretation does not then see the typical processes of normative adaptation as merely epiphenomena of upward mobility, but rather as strategic forms of behaviour in the face of rigid occupational barriers to mobility. This thesis fits easily with Stone's data:

> Of the 60 salesmen interviewed, the 30 who indicated that mobility or promotion considerations were of central importance to them displayed the following characteristics in their interviews: (1) loyalty to employers, (2) a tendency to accept the beliefs of those above them.[60]

In this case, concrete experience, suggesting the possibility or probability of factual promotion, obviously played no part. An excerpt from one of Stone's interviews shows graphically how the individual almost instrumentally accepts in advance the fundamentally new attitudes which he sees as part of the higher role he wishes to gain:

[59] Cf. D. Lockwood, *The blackcoated worker* (London 1958), 6off.; D. Claessens, J. Fuhrmann, G. Harfiel and H. Zirvas, *Angestellte und Arbeiter in der Betriebspyramide*, ed. O. Stammer (Berlin 1960); C. W. Mills, *White collar* (New York 1956).
[60] Stone, 'Mobility factors . . .', 60.

If a guy is going to become a manager, he can't help but think like the management does. That means he is going to accept the capitalistic system. Now I have lots of sympathies for the labor unions and what they are trying to do for people. But if you are going to move into management, you just have to think the way they do. That means, you can't be in conflict with the viewpoint of the people you are under.[61]

There is no reason why, as Stone believes to be the case, the mere existence of vertical mobility should cause this almost virtuoso willingness to adapt—by itself this factor could not explain the remarkable immunity of the control group of manual workers[62] to this sort of occupational pressure to conformity. On the contrary, it seems that a cultural stratification which occurs outside the organization reproduces itself inside it in the process of organizational status allocation and mobility: the middle class's achievement motivation is transformed into rewarded loyalty, while for the manual working class similar adaptive mechanisms cannot override the continual experience of a *collective* conflict situation.

Extrafunctional loyalty, then, is not just a learned phenomenon accompanying upward mobility. Instead it is above all something which the individual can use in vaguely defined mobility channels or in ones which are blocked by discontinuities and dead ends. Extrafunctional loyalty is therefore deliberately acquired and utilized to gain promotion. In a study which will be discussed again later, Dalton puts forward the same interpretation:

Absence of a sharply defined mode of ascent encouraged the managers to work for more subtle means of elevating themselves.... The managerial search for mobility ladders sharpened their sensitivity to the attitudes and attributes of superiors and induced competition to please.[63]

The discussion so far of various empirical studies has necessarily been incomplete and unsystematic. Nonetheless, it has yielded evidence to suggest that in the present phase of industrial-bureaucratic work, occupational role identities and mobility strategies are increasingly built upon extrafunctional or peripheral role elements. The following section will ask whether, and to what extent, the institutionalized selection and promotion mechanisms of formal organizations operate in a complementary fashion, i.e. whether they too are based on extrafunctional criteria. Before we do this however, three problems have to be discussed, even though there is no empirical material available which enable them to be completely resolved: the problem of job satisfaction, the importance of the work role relative to other roles, and the professionalization thesis.

---

[61] *Ibid.*
[62] Cf. *ibid.*, 61ff.
[63] Cf. M. Dalton, 'Informal factors in career achievement', *AJS* 56 (1950), 407–14, esp. 414; *idem, Men who manage* (New York 1959), 148–93; Coates and Pellegrin, 'Executives and supervisors: informal factors . . .'.

One of the most frequently-confirmed theses of industrial and organizational sociology is the tight positive relationship between status in the organization and job satisfaction: the higher the position within the organizational hierarchy, the greater the job satisfaction of its occupant.[64] At first sight this link seems to be of little interest: it is normally explained by the way in which a high position ensures a higher level of satisfaction of physiological, psychological and cultural needs. It is argued that physiological stresses, such as noise, dust and heat, are greater in the lower positions filled by the directly productive workers, just as the occupants of such positions experience greater dissatisfaction because of the nervous stress of the repetitive character of the work task and the boredom of routine work processes. Finally it is assumed that in these positions a fundamental need for 'self-actualization'[65] is continually frustrated, so that work dissatisfaction is perpetuated. By contrast, the situation of clerical workers and management is claimed to be completely different, for the stresses inherent in the position are less, and the chances of satisfying basic psychological and cultural needs are correspondingly greater, so that job satisfaction is higher and more stable.

However, there are two possible objections to this sketched explanatory model of the typical distribution pattern of job satisfaction. Firstly, it is not really a sociological model at all, for it rests on the psychologistic assumption that people in all social strata have the same fixed needs and that the extent to which these needs are satisfied at work depends purely upon the rank of the job within the organization's hierarchy.

This sort of argument obscures the fact that there is no *direct* causal connection between the objective variable of work conditions and the subjective variable of job satisfaction. Instead, the link itself is first always created by the intervention of specific expectations, value systems and self-conceptions of the workers. The linkage, in other words, is subjectively mediated.[66] It follows from this argument that with any given work conditions the subjective level of job satisfaction does not arise 'from itself', but only through the 'filter' of specific expectations and occupational role identities. Higher or lower job satisfaction would then be caused by the relative difference between the group-specific expectations, which have become part of the individual's understanding of his role, and the objective work conditions.

W. Baldamus[67] has applied this thesis to the analysis of jobs in

---

[64] Cf. V. H. Vroom, *Work and motivation* (New York 1964), 129, which also gives many additional references.
[65] Cf. *ibid.*
[66] Cf. Institut für Sozialforschung, *Betriebsklima* (Frankfurt a.M. 1955).
[67] Cf. W. Baldamus, *Efficiency and effort* (London 1961).

industrial production. He criticizes the traditional industrial psychology approach, in which

> it was assumed, without evidence, that effort (and similar phenomena such as fatigue) is a linear function of the physical energy consumed in working.[68]

He insists, in opposition to this mechanistic thesis, on the 'contrast of objective work realities and subjective deprivations.'[69] Whether 'stressful' work conditions are actually reflected in the subjective experience of tiredness, monotony or boredom at work depends not on the objective characteristics of the work situation itself, but rather on how the workers define their work situation and their role in it. Depending therefore on how the work roles are defined, aspects of the work situation which are stressful from an 'objective' physiological and psychological point of view can have a nonexistent or even a positive influence on job satisfaction. Baldamus demonstrates this mechanism through the example of very repetitive forms of work, pointing out that these in no way necessarily lead to a feeling of work weariness, but can on the contrary contain the relaxing element of 'traction':

> it is a feeling of being pulled along by the inertia inherent in a particular activity. The experience is pleasant and may therefore function as a relief from tedium.[70]

Certainly, there is a total difference between pointing out the *possibility* of such reinterpretations of the objective work situation and Gehlen's cynical anthropological *normative* conception, which postulates 'the transformation of work into habit with its own adequate intrinsic reward'.[71] One question can summarize the second objection which has to be made to the outlined explanatory model of the linkage between social status and job satisfaction within organizational hierarchies: in the different layers of the hierarchy, are the 'objective' physiological and psychological stresses or rewards of work really different enough to explain by themselves the rapid rise of job satisfaction with increasing status? For a broad middle sector of the hierarchy one cannot demonstrate that such differences do actually exist, either for the material rewards of work or for the typical working conditions of manual and clerical workers. On the contrary, there is strong evidence that working conditions in factories and offices are slowly but nonetheless continually becoming more and more alike.[72] The comparative indus-

[68] *Ibid.*, 51.
[69] *Ibid.*
[70] *Ibid.*, 59.
[71] A. Gehlen, *Urmensch und Spätkultur* (Bonn 1956).
[72] Cf. H. P. Bahrdt, 'Arbeitssoziologische Aspekte des technischen Fortschritts in der Industrieverwaltung', *Hmb. Jb.* 5 (1960), 58–68.

trial sociological study carried out by Claessens *et al.* could find no dramatic difference between the working conditions of manual workers and those of large sections of the clerical work force. This same conclusion is implied in our thesis, namely that 'work with symbols' allows less opportunity for demonstrable objectification or self-actualization than 'work with things', even though for the manual worker such work too is indirect, owing to technological mediation. Given the far-reaching tendencies towards equalization of objective work stresses and work rewards, the 'mechanistic' explanation of the connection between status and job satisfaction becomes implausible.

The alternative explanation which follows is as yet not backed up by much empirical evidence and therefore must to a certain extent remain speculative. The question is how, when it is impossible to find 'objective' differences in stress and chances of satisfaction between jobs, it is still possible for the different self-conceptions and role-specific need-dispositions decisive for the level of job satisfaction nonetheless to occur. We can approach a solution to this question if we take the explanatory variable to be, not the working conditions, but rather the group-specific need-dispositions (or standards of work satisfaction). If we do this, then the problem can be reformulated as follows: how does it come about that the higher-status groups develop occupational role identities and interpretations of their needs which are more suited to the objective facts of their work situation, and which therefore lead to a lower experience of failure or deprivation?

The results of the previous discussion allow the question to be answered at two levels. Firstly, in terms of the strategies of individuals oriented to upward mobility and, secondly in terms of the interest of organizations in mechanisms of status allocation which helps to maintain the stability of the status quo.

If people's aspirations are for an individual improvement in their social status (as has been demonstrated to be the case for, for example, the American middle class,[73] but at the same time discontinuous-qualification structures and rigid barriers to mobility within the organization prevent these aspirations from being directly channelled into instrumental behaviour (i.e. into 'central' role elements or categories of performance), then there occurs a ritualized objectification of particular norms and role elements of the work process. This process is similar in structure to that whereby bureaucratic behaviour becomes autonomous. In a situation in which objective technological and organizational determinants of work make the demonstration of individual *goal-conforming* per-

[73] For the extensive literature on the 'achievement motive' and the 'standards of excellence' of the middle classes, cf. the studies listed under footnote 26, p.58

formance ability difficult, then the competition for recognition of the productive attributes of the individual occurs in a different area: instead of only governing the practice of an occupation, work norms become dissociated from the instrumental context of the work process and become the subject of independent motivation.[74] This mechanism explains the affinity of standards of work satisfaction with factual work conditions in those cultural strata characterized by high status ambitions—one method of improving one's status is to demonstrate the needs and life style which suit the normative system which claims validity in the work situation.

From the point of view of the maintenance of the stability of organizations, it is equally important that the higher the position in the hierarchy, the more the occupational need dispositions of the workers coincide with the chances of satisfying them. This occurs partly through the process of ritualization which has just been mentioned, and partly through the mechanisms of status ascription and promotion which the organization controls—these will be discussed in the next section of this chapter.

How important it is that job satisfaction should be higher in the higher-status groups is shown by the fact that, in the upper areas of the hierarchy, control over the organization's power resources increases, while the effectiveness of *external* control over role-conforming behaviour decreases. Both factors make it necessary to employ in higher positions people with need dispositions and standards of satisfaction which can be fulfilled as completely as possible by the available gratifications. If needs and available gratifications by contrast did not coincide, then there would be the danger that deviant motivations would develop, manifesting themselves as a disturbance of the organized system of domination or as failure in work roles which are closed to the intervention of direct control from 'above'. This interpretation of the origin of job satisfaction enables us to take the linkage of organizational status and 'job satisfaction' as a further proof of the extent to which 'peripheral' need-dispositions influence the occupational role identity and are used to supplement objective criteria of status.

Another argument for this thesis is suggested by the astonishing influence of occupational roles on the determination of pre-occupational, post-occupational and non-occupational roles—the higher the occupational role in the hierarchy the greater its influence. At the level of research techniques this is reflected in the fact that in all industrial societies occupation and occupational group is taken as the most powerful explanatory variable in attitudinal and behavioural research studies on such completely 'work-distant' areas

[74] Cf. also A. Gehlen, 'Problems einer soziologischen Handlungslehre', in C. Brinkmann (ed.), *Soziologie und Leben* (Tübingen 1952), 28–59.

of life as politics, religion, sexuality, leisure behaviour, etc.[75] The stability of this linkage is astonishing for two reasons. Firstly, given such trends in industrial capitalist societies as the levelling out of the differences in the work situations of many occupations (a trend demonstrable by industrial sociology), urbanization, declining differences in the average length of education and the increasing similarity of the conditions of production, one could expect occupation to be losing its importance as *the* differentiating characteristic of individual role systems. Secondly, one could hypothesize that the influence of the work role on other roles is *removed* by the worker's increasingly technically and organizationally mediated relationship to his object of work, the partial and specialized demands of many work roles, the reduced demonstrability of occupational work and the reduced share of work time in individuals' life history.

The concept of peripheral role identity dissolves the apparent contradiction between the fact that work has at least retained its function for the individual's overall self-conception, while at the same time placing quantitively and qualitatively only limited demands on people. Certainly it has to be admitted that in any organization based on a division of labour, the importance of work was never restricted to providing the individual with a means of livelihood and to confirming his own 'ability' in the solution of the organization's goals. Work also provided a series of other gratifications, of which the most important was clearly the relatively stable social relationships and informal groupings of the workplace.[76] However, it is not immediately clear why functional equivalents outside the work organization could not support and mould the personal identity when the central elements of the work role can no longer fulfil this function in the same way as before. In a study concerned with those functions of the work role which go beyond instrumental motivations, Morse and Weiss[77] convincingly reject the assumption that the importance of work is decreasing in relation to other sources of identity. According to them it is still pre-eminently the work role sector which

> gives ... a feeling of being tied into the larger society, of having something to do, of having a purpose in life. These other functions which working serves are evidently not seen as available in nonwork activities.

[75] This is pointed out by L. Wilensky in a study of the relationship between the work role and role sectors which are distant from work. 'Occupational cultures (rooted in common tasks, work schedules, job training and career patterns) are sometimes better predictors of behaviour than both social class and pre-job experience.' H. L. Wilensky, 'Orderly career patterns and social participation: the impact of work history on social integration in the middle class', *ASR* 26 (1961), 521–39, here 521.

[76] Cf. Slocum, *Occupational careers*; Vroom, *Work and motivation*, 43.

[77] N. C. Morse and R. S. Weiss, 'The function and meaning of work and the job', *ASR* 20 (1955), 191–8.

F

The unique characteristic of the work role is its ability to crystallize and thus to shape groups of motives which originate outside work, and Morse and Weiss further confirm that this increases in the higher status groups.

Similarly, in a study of the rehabilitation chances of schizophrenics, Ozzie G. Simmons assumes that

> in view of the central place that work occupies in the life of the individual, it must play a strategic part in helping him to establish his identity, and it becomes highly charged as a symbol of meaningful life.[78]

E contrario, this thesis is supported also by Bakke, who shows that unemployment, quite apart from its effects on material living conditions, disorganizes the entire role system of the individual.[79]

Given that work roles are characterized by the fact that their functional requirements are becoming ever more specialized, all these results can only be explained by the effectiveness of an occupational role identity which is built up from extrafunctional role elements. The work role's de facto pre-eminence can be explained by ritualistic identification with, and loyalty (based on mobility orientation) to, the dominant value system of the work organization—in short, by the growth of the work role into a lifestyle.

Finally, the professionalization thesis is interesting for the problem of extrafunctional occupational role identity. The area of occupational roles known as 'the professions' shows particularly clearly the process in which the regulatory norms of the work process are transformed into demonstrable symbols of an occupational caste, symbols which can then in turn be used as the basis for claims to status. The 'professions' are in fact an extreme example of a more general tendency—the occupational group combines relatively high claims to status with a monopoly of effective power to evaluate the individual member, so that the demonstrability of individual talent in the central elements of the work role is at a minimum.[80] Outside the group of professional experts no one can judge the level to which the occupational task has been fulfilled. Nonetheless, the individual and collective claims to status made by the group's members can ultimately only be successful if they are granted legitimacy by people, such as clients or superiors, who are unqualified to judge the professional occupational work. In this dilemma[81]

[78] Ozzie G. Simmons, *Work and mental illness* (New York 1965), 15.

[79] E. W. Bakke, *Citizens without work* (New Haven 1940); for the situation in five occupations during and after the end of the work role, see E. A. Friedmann and R. J. Havinghurst, *The meaning of work and retirement* (Chicago 1954).

[80] Cf. E. Greenwood, 'Attributes of a profession', in Nosow and Form, *Man, work and society*, 206–18.

[81] Cf. the analysis of J. Bensman and J. Gerver, 'Towards a sociology of expertness', *Soc. Forc.* 32 (1953–4), 226–35.

the shift to peripheral elements of the occupational role is almost unavoidable—services can only be made credible and exchanged for high-status rewards if their creation is mystified by stylizing regulatory norms or functionally completely unimportant symbols into an impressive image, one which sometimes includes the very language and clothes of the occupation.

It is in this way that the 'regulative code of ethics' of a 'profession' and the demonstration of a 'professional culture' (Greenwood) are used to further individual and collective status claims. This model derives from the academically-trained professions, and it has so far not been adequately empirically demonstrated how far it applies beyond this area. However, there is no general reason why it should not be applied to all expert roles.

Instead of using a substantive criterion, such as the amount of knowledge accumulated, to define expert roles, we can use that of specialization. This leads to an investigation of the extent to which qualifications are tied to a particular workplace (or put the other way round, the extent to which qualifications cannot be transferred to other workplaces) and also of the extent to which qualified personal control can be exercised over the occupant of the position.[82] According to this transferability criterion, positions such as porter or storekeeper then have a large amount of expert character. If we operationalize expertise in this way, then it becomes plausible that 'islands of expertise', occupied by 'relative experts', can be found at all levels of the structures of large organizations. These 'experts' are only able to justify their claims to relative status and their aspirations for mobility by demonstrating their identity with the help of those very norms and symbols which are not at the centre of their work functions, but which are however widely recognized. In this context it is interesting to note that various authors have in fact pointed out the widespread tendency towards 'professionalization', especially of the roles of skilled workers.[83]

We now return to the theoretical considerations which introduced this chapter. The technological and organizational work conditions which have been described all suggest that peripheral role elements are being made the basis of occupational role identity, and that these elements of the role are strategically utilized in processes of upward mobility. The empirical discussion so far has confirmed this. Work conditions also suggest that the relevant authorities in organizations have to use extrafunctional criteria to select for

[82] These two criteria have already been discussed through the concept of the 'discontinuous qualification structure'—cf. chapter 1 above.
[83] Cf. N. N. Foote, 'The professionalization of labor in Detroit', *AJS* 58 (1953), 371–80; idem, 'The movement from jobs to careers in American industry', *Transactions of the 2nd World Congress of Sociology* (London 1956), II, 30–40; H. M. Vollmer and D. L. Mills, 'Nuclear technology and the professionalization of labor', in Vollmer and Mills (eds.), *Professionalization* (Englewood Cliffs, NJ, 1966).

recruitment and promotion. The individual's definition of his occupational role, as stimulated by his status aspirations, would then be paralleled by organizational measures: since individual performance as a contribution to the product cannot be objectified or demonstrated, and since within discontinuous qualification structures individual performance cannot be utilized as a rational criterion for movement between hierarchical positions, peripheral role elements are replacing central ones at both the individual and the organizational levels.

4   Extrafunctional determinants of recruitment and promotion in formal organizations

If our assumptions as to the nature of 'specialization' and 'discontinuous qualification structure' are correct, then it is in fact astonishing that there is any internal mobility at all which is anything more than a movement through a series of temporary positions on the way to a final occupational role. From an economic point of view, any other form of intra-organizational ascent (such as a career path from representative to distribution planner to sales manager) is inexpedient for two reasons: (1) specialized knowledge acquired in one position is not transferable to another and so becomes redundant, (2) since the qualifications required for the new positions are not simply extensions of the ones already acquired, they necessitate costly and time-consuming retraining processes (as opposed to simply training). Given the characteristics of the division of labour that have already been pointed out, and leaving aside the employee's own ambitions for promotion, one has to ask how it can make sense for the dominant interests in the organization to institutionalize or at least permit processes of mobility.

Within American sociology there has in fact been an extensive discussion over whether this internal mobility (i.e. mobility inside one generation and inside one organization) is declining.[84] Apart from the already mentioned economic and business administration reasons, certain tendencies in the overall social development of industrial capitalist systems also provide evidence that suggests the decline of internal mobility. Chinoy, however, in summarizing the arguments comes to the conclusion that at the present stage of research it is not possible to make any clear decision in favour of the immobility thesis. Pre-sociological everyday experience also sug-

[84] Cf. J. O. Hertzler, 'Some tendencies toward a closed class system in the United States', *Soc. Forc.* 30 (1952), 313–23; S. M. Lipset and R. Bendix, 'Social mobility and occupational career patterns', *AJS* 57 (1952), 366–74, 494–504; E. Chinoy, 'Social mobility trends in the United States', *ASR* 20 (1955), 180–86; R. C. Stone, 'Factory organization and vertical mobility', *ASR* 18 (1953), 28–35.

gests that these developmental tendencies have not yet completely abolished internal mobility.

In his standard work on labour economics, Reynolds confirms what we have assumed—the dependency of mobility on the technologically-determined workplace structure.[85] He assumes that internal mobility is greatest where 'the division of labor is not marked by sharp discontinuities.' This condition is however no longer true for the advanced areas of industrial production: the qualifications of, for instance, 'unskilled workers', 'semiskilled machine operators' and 'maintenance and repair men' have lost their technical continuity:

> They are separated by sharp discontinuities in the division of labor. Little or nothing that any one worker does in any of the three classes prepares him to assume the work task assigned in a higher class.[86]

Given the disadvantages of internal mobility from a business administration point of view, what are the relative advantages which nonetheless ensure that upward movements continue to take place within the organizational hierarchy? We intend to answer this question with the following hypothesis as a first approximation: in task-discontinuous hierarchies, mobility necessitates the cost of retraining processes and the redundancy of specialized knowledge. Mobility therefore occurs to the extent that these relative disadvantages are more than counterbalanced by the relative advantages deriving from the upwardly mobile individual's contribution to the stability of the organization's system of domination through his loyalty and conformist identification.[87] A negative proof of the influence of this equation is that the intra-organizational promotion rate is lowest for those positions in which specialization (and therefore the cost of promotion) is highest.[88] This applies especially for experts and academically educated employees with a long training period, since

> An institution invests time, money and energy in the training of its recruits and members which it cannot afford to let to go to waste.[89]

The organization's interest in immobility is additionally protected by increasing the subjective costs which the employee would incur if he transferred to another employer. Measures to achieve this

[85] Cf. L. Reynolds, *The Structure of labor markets* (New York 1951), 139–54.
[86] *Ibid.*, cited by H. M. Gitelman, *Ind. and Lab. Rel. Rev.* 20 (1966), 50–65.
[87] This thesis applies only to 'distance mobility' under constant external conditions, not to 'demand mobility' (i.e. mobility which occurs because of changing relationships in the number of workplaces). Cf. N. Rogoff, 'Recent trends in occupational mobility', in P. K. Hatt and J. Reiss (eds.), *Cities and society* (2nd edn, New York 1957), 432–45.
[88] Cf. Blau, *Exchange and power in social life.*
[89] H. S. Becker and A. L. Strauss, 'Careers, personality and adult socialization', *AJS* 62 (1956–7), 253–63, here 254.

include age-related social welfare benefits and company shareholding schemes, as well as specific clauses in the work contract.[90]

The blockage of mobility out of a given position is only one side of the tendency towards the reduction of internal mobility: the other is that personnel for higher positions are frequently recruited not 'from below' but 'from outside'—i.e. recruitment is linked to formalized educational processes. Stone found this tendency confirmed for all levels of management:

> Managers will be drawn from some other source than worker levels, i.e. will never have occupied the status of workers. . . . There has been an increase in the ratio of college to non-college trained managers.[91]

This tendency towards external recruitment also contributes to reducing the chances of internal mobility. External recruitment not only functions to make available formalized specialist knowledge for the corresponding work tasks, but also has a positive function, since, through pre-occupational socialization processes in school, technical college and university, it equips the aspirant to a position with normative orientations and ideological loyalties which better match the dominant interests of the organization than those which would be provided by recruitment 'from below'. The relative weight of these two technological and normative functions of external recruitment cannot be exactly estimated.

As well as the blockage of specialists' promotion and the fact of external recruitment for higher positions, there is a third mechanism which plays an important part in the immobilization of typical occupational destinies within organizational hierarchies. I am referring here to the phenomenon of 'ideological status differentiation' first described by C. Dreyfuss.[92] Dreyfuss describes a type of mobility which can be seen especially amongst clerical workers. Here it is a question of 'advancement' from one hierarchical position to another, when these positions are not in fact vertically stratified at all, but rather 'objectively' lie on the same hierarchical level: in terms of their specific work tasks there is no difference between the two positions, nor does the higher one offer larger material rewards, more prestige, autonomy or authority than the one from which the person has just been promoted. The 'higher value' of the status is only a symbolically-simulated one, in that for instance the workplace is fitted out with status symbols (office equipment, own towel, own telephone, nameplate etc.), while the substance of the work and the material rewards remain the same.

[90] Cf. Hertzler, 'Some tendencies towards a closed class system . . .', 318.
[91] Stone, 'Factory organization and vertical mobility', 29.
[92] C. Dreyfuss, 'Prestige grading: a mechanism of control', in Merton *et al.*, *Reader in bureaucracy* (New York 1962), 259–64; cf. also H. P. Bahrdt, *Industriebürokratie* (Stuttgart 1958), 114ff.

It follows that the thesis of the effectiveness of extrafunctional criteria for promotion and recruitment can only be demonstrated for those mobility processes which have remained untouched by the three mechanisms of immobility described above. On the continuum between central and peripheral role elements (or between functional and extrafunctional elements) there are four types of criteria for promotion and selection:

1   standards of success
2   educational standards
3   ideological orientations
4   ascriptive characteristics.

Each of these criteria is more loosely linked than the one before it to the central role elements. Since the studies which will be examined here do not discuss these criteria separately or systematically, we have first to show why they can be held to have an 'extrafunctional' character. In particular, this would seem to be difficult to justify for the first two.

1   *Standards of success.* If standards of success are to operate as criteria for advancement, this means that those people who occupy the lower position A with over-average success are seen as suitable to fill the higher position B. In many traditional organizations this schema of advancement has a rational sense, namely wherever the two positions A and B have a core of common tasks and of technical rules through which these tasks are fulfilled. However, wherever this criterion is not met, then there are three objections to the rationality of 'standards of success' as a criterion for promotion:

(a) Organizational and technological reasons can prevent something such as 'success', ability or productivity being visible and adequately comparable with another position. Indeed, forms of work such as 'team cooperation'[93] make it impossible to locate the success of any one individual, even if the limitations on 'social visibility' were to be removed. In such work situations the success criterion is ideological: it purports to ascribe to separate individuals something which has only been created as the indivisible total product of the work group.

(b) The contradiction between cooperative production and the simultaneous retention of the individualistic 'success evaluation' can only be resolved by elevating a peripheral sector of work behaviour into the criterion for success instead of the individual's 'contribution to the product'. Individual evaluation would then be by the worker's self-presentation instead of by his fulfilment of his

[93] H. Popitz, H. P. Bahrdt, A. Jüres and J. Kesting, *Technik und Industriearbeit* (Stuttgart 1957).

work tasks. In short, presenting oneself as wanting success would become the symbolic substitute for performance that has now become undefinable and abstract. However, ability in self-presentation is clearly a peripheral element of occupational behaviour.

(c) Even in conditions which allow the correct ascription of success according to *central* role elements, the rationality of 'success' as a criterion for promotion has to be challenged: namely, the less the work tasks of positions A and B overlap, the less value 'success' in A has an indicator of 'qualification' for B. Yet precisely this noncontinuity is the defining characteristic of task-discontinuous hierarchies.

The less continuity there is between the requirements of position A and position B, the more unreliable and therefore the more senseless is promotion which depends on success, even in positions in which 'success' is manifested *only* in individual ability.

2   *Educational standards.* There are also some necessary objects to the argument that the educational standards used as criteria for recruitment and promotion are rational, since they are only concerned with central elements of the work role. Summarized in the form of theses these objections are:

(a)   The preceding discussion has already shown that formalized educational processes transfer normative elements and ideological orientations as well as merely technical rules. The criterion of educational standards refers to both classes of rules—it does not therefore only measure only functional role elements.

(b)   The alleged congruity between the content of education and the functional requirements specific to each position is basically dubious. Deviations from this congruity occur because (1) only a tiny proportion of the acquired productive ability and knowledge is actually needed in the concrete tasks of the work place,[94] i.e. much of the content of education is functionally superfluous and serves to symbolize the status claims of individuals or occupational castes. The best known example of this is academic 'luxury knowledge'. On the other hand (2) not all the role elements which are functional in large bureaucratic organizations are formalizable *outside* the organization. There are arguments which suggest that the tendency towards specialization is leading to an increasing difference between educational knowledge and functional occupational knowledge. Institutionalized forms of post-entry training are increasing at all levels within organizations—witness all the forms of apprenticeship and traineeship in industry, education, law etc.[95] The

[94] U. Gembardt, 'Akademische Ausbildung und Beruf', *KZfSS* 11 (1959) 223–45.

[95] Once educational and occupational knowledge diverge, then educational standards become less important as a measure of individual occupational ability. The 'job-nearness' of the actual occupational education is documented by Slocum for the USA: 'The majority of the nation's workers

appointments pages of the big daily newspapers show that most of the authorities looking for workers in the labour market do not define the labour power they want only in terms of references and educational career, but (at least) also through experience in pre- cisely-defined areas and workplaces. The same is suggested by the working-in period which is frequently offered to the new occupant of a post. Similarly, the reforms proposed by industry for the educational system require that as much training as possible should be displaced from institutions of technical and higher education into the immediate vicinity of the work situation.[96]

(c) Even where the growing discrepancy between educational knowledge and occupational qualification has not devalued 'educa- tional standards' as a criterion for the evaluation of ability for a specific occupation, it still improbable that the employers are able to gain an adequate picture of the functional content of those educational processes and institutions whose alumni they prefer or discriminate against. Often educational standards are only kept because they correspond to the employers' needs for prestige. This aspect is particularly important in the USA. For instance, if the alumni of particular colleges, military academies[97] and universities are preferred or discriminated against, clearly this does not happen because of the particular functional abilities which the institution transmits—not only is the employer not normally capable of making any such qualified assessment, but also exams and references would be a better index of the functional abilities. Instead, discrimination or preference is based on the cultural peculiarities and the specific traditions of the different institutions.

3   *Ideologies.* The extrafunctional character of this category of criteria is obvious. Regulatory norms integrated into the individual's lifestyle, readiness to adapt, avoidance of conflict, loyalty to the dominant interests in the organization, acceptance of the cultural pattern of the dominant groups, ability for anticipatory socializa- tion etc.—in short more or less abstract adaptability—here make up the criterion for assessment by which the individual's mobility chances are measured.[98]

---

with less than three years of college reported that they had not learned their occupational roles through formal education: 56 per cent had learned on the job, to some extent by company training courses, but mainly through experience supplemented by instruction from supervisors, or by learning from a friend or relative.' Slocum, *Occupational careers*, 147–8.

[96] Cf. H. Dichgans, *Die Dauer der Ausbildung für akademische Berufe: Schriftenreihe des Stifterverbandes zur Förderung der Wissenschaft* (Essen 1963).

[97] Cf. the description by C. W. Mills of the recruitment mechanisms of his three 'directorates', in particular of the military. C. W. Mills, *The power elite* (New York 1958).

[98] Cf. G. Bensman and A. Vidich, 'Power cliques in bureaucratic society', *Soc. Res.* 29 (1962), 467–74.

4   *Ascriptive characteristics.* Two types can be distinguished within this group of organizational criteria. Ascriptive criteria are based on (a) natural categories used as characteristics or (b) 'institutional links'. Evaluative measures such as age, sex, skin colour, ethnic origin belong to the group of *natural categories*. By contrast, the mechanism of institutional linkage occurs when membership of an *institution* outside work becomes decisive for occupational destiny: examples of this are criteria such as religion, familial status and membership of parties, trade unions or organizations. The characteristics on which the first type of criteria are based cannot be voluntarily changed, in broad contrast to those of the second type.

To a certain extent the criterion of seniority[99] occupies a special position in this group, both because of its apparent rationality and because of its frequent use. Certainly, under specific conditions this criterion can represent central role elements, namely when it is assumed that abilities and productive knowledge accumulate in the course of a particular employment, making the person with the longest service the most qualified member of the hierarchy. However, the limits of this argument are clear. If the technologically-defined work situation changes relatively frequently, then seniority loses its value as a measure of differences in technical competence. On the contrary, retaining the principle of seniority in this case can lead to delays in adaptation and to 'structural conservatism'. When this happens, the criterion loses any validity for work tasks which have to be fulfilled by obedience to regulatory norms rather than by technical rules accumulated through experience, for there is no reason at all why the former should increase in effectiveness with increasing seniority.

There is an important distinction that has to be made between the form of ascription under discussion here and its pre-industrial form. Unlike the medieval estate system, in the bureaucratic organizations of industrial society natural categories and institutional links are not used to justify a status within the system of division of labour because of *legally*-sanctioned barriers to mobility. Instead, natural categories and institutional links fulfil merely symbolic functions in a form of status allocation that is itself basically contractual. Ascriptive mechanisms refer to specific roles and systems of norms whose scope can be relatively reliably defined by natural categories or by roles in other institutions the roles and norms are the basis of ascription and not the natural categories themselves. Natural categories, then, only *symbolize* elements of age, sex or national roles, and as regulatory norms or extrafunctional orientations these elements have important functions in the work organiza-

[99] Cf. Fürstenburg, *Probleme der Lohnstruktur*; Slocum, *Occupational careers*, 255ff.; Bahrdt, *Industriebürokratie*, 110ff.

tion. This ascriptive principle of selection operates simultaneously 'beneath' the legal status restrictions typical of pre-industrial societies.

Two forms of ascriptive recruitment can be distinguished—positive ascription selects conforming orientations, while negative ascription rejects deviant normative systems. For purposes of clarification this distinction can be combined with that between natural categories and institutional links in a two-by-two table. The following illustrations of the different types of ascription use examples drawn from the subsequent discussion of empirical research results.

| | *Ascriptive status criteria* | |
	Natural categories	Institutional links
Positive	Discrimination in favour of women	Discrimination in favour of members of own party
Negative	Discrimination against Southern Europeans	Discrimination against members of religious minorities

One of the most important examples of the use of natural categories as symbols of typical normative systems is the sex-specific division of labour. Under the work conditions of advanced technology, it is clear that the explanation for the 'feminization' of large occupational groups is not that women are physically better suited than men to these occupations (or, alternatively, that men concentrate on those tasks where the physical requirements rule out the employment of women). The explanation is rather that the culturally-defined female sex role contains elements which can be particularly usefully employed as regulatory norms and organizational loyalties in 'feminine' occupations. In the USA the occupations which are typical female ones[100] demonstrate the ascriptive selection at work at the level of the whole society: without exception these occupations can be seen as occupational forms of the 'real' female role, that of mother, spouse and housewife.

The sex-specific division of labour in the factory has been described by Warner:[101]

> Women's jobs were primarily evolutions of tasks which they have traditionally performed in the home—knitting, stitching, washing, cleaning and packing.

[100] 'Dieticians, nutritionists, librarians, nurses, social workers, elementary school teachers, stenographers, typists and secretaries, telephone operators, book-keepers, cashiers, dressmakers and seamstresses, private household workers, hospital attendants, practical nurses, midwives, waitresses.' Slocum, *Occupational careers*, 101.
[101] W. L. Warner, *The social system of a modern factory* (New Haven 1945), 90ff.

Taking this study by Warner of the work force of a shoe factory as an example, we can define more exactly the difference between regulatory norms which still have some unintended practical content, and completely extrafunctional orientations. In their objective function in this sense, the 'female skills' which have been transferred from the housewife role to the workplace are closer to regulatory norms than to extrafunctional orientations. The existence of such 'female skills', however, is not the only reason for the existing sex-specific division of labour. Women are also characterized by greater submissiveness to authority, lower wage claims and a tendency to avoid conflict: these *extrafunctional* elements of the occupational role also derive from the position of women in the middleclass family system. As such they directly benefit the maintenance of the relations of domination in the organization, without making any contribution at all to the 'productivity' of work:

> Management can pay low rates to women employees without arousing any great resentment on the part of workers, male or female ... Foremen feel ... that large groups of women operatives do not constitute the potential serious threat to the operation of controls that men operatives do. This is because women seem not to develop the social solidarities in their working relations that men do. ... Lack of solidarity among women was mentioned as one of the managerial considerations that increase their desirability as employees.[102]

At the level of the labour market as a whole, the extent of ascriptive occupational distribution has in fact increased: in the USA the proportion of workers in the 'clerical and kindred workers' census category who were women rose between 1940 and 1970 by 36 per cent to a total of 73 per cent.[103]

The opposite case of 'negative' ascription occurs when the application of ascriptive categories prevents employees with deviant orientations from attaining particular jobs. The same difference between negative and positive ascription also occurs in the case of ascription on the basis of institutional links.

Here one objection has to be anticipated: it might seem that the claimed growth of ascriptive status allocation is contradicted by the frequently-observed increased use of scientifically routinized tests (usually of a psychological sort) for the recruitment and promotion of personnel—it could be claimed that such predictive tests focus very sophisticatedly on precisely the functional elements of the work role.

If this were the case, then obviously it would contradict the idea that ascriptive criteria are becoming more widespread. However, there is little in favour of this argument, since attitude tests and occupational suitability tests only have the function of providing a measure of an administratively-fixed minimum level of qualifica-

102 *Ibid.*, 97.
103 Calculated from Slocum, *Occupational careers*, 102.

tion, and this standard does not therefore have to coincide with the factual requirements of the job. Even when it does, the tests have a very limited predictive value: the employees' previously developed self-conception (i.e. the totality of norms and attitudes actually *followed* at work) can prevent the qualifications which the test measures from ever being actualized in the work situation. The development of self-conceptions is a social-psychological process which reflects concrete and situationally specific interaction with the organization's structure of domination. A predictive schema which is based on individual psychology can therefore only to a very limited extent grasp a social process like this: even if such scientific evaluation procedures are adequate to the task set them, important determinants of actual behaviour at work escape them. For this reason Mayo himself criticized the naive use of psychological occupational tests:

> The belief that the behavior of an individual within the factory can be predicted before employment upon the basis of a laborious and minute examination by tests of his technical and other capacities is mainly, when not wholly, mistaken. Examination of his developed social skills and general adaptability might give better results. The usual situation is that after employment the relation to 'the team' will go far to determine the use he makes of such capacities as he has developed.[104]

Yet even Mayo's proposed alternative, testing the individual's adaptability, is equally dubious. Adaptability as an element of the occupational role identity only first develops and is continually modified at the workplace itself. The pattern of distribution of reasons for dismissal shows that criteria which have nothing directly to do with fulfilment of the work task are important for 'success' in the job:

> Countless studies have shown that inability to get on with workmates and foremen is a more frequent reason for dismissal than inadequate work.[105]

The discussion which follows of empirical studies does not sharply distinguish between the four groups of extrafunctional criteria which operate in recruitment and promotion in work organizations, since none of them, especially that of success standards, has been studied separately and systematically.

All industrial and organizational sociological studies agree that

[104] E. Mayo, *The social problems of an industrial civilization* (Cambridge, Mass., 1945), 111; cf. also W. H. Whyte, *The organization man* (London 1960).
[105] D. C. Miller and W. H. Form, *Industrial sociology: the sociology of work organization* (New York 1955), 208.

the decisive authority for ascent within the organization is the immediately superior position in the hierarchy.[106] As far as the superior's assessment of success is concerned, there is an interesting and undiscussed subsidiary finding in a study by Foa of a textile factory.[107] The study shows a connection between the level of the foreman's personal familiarity with the workers and his own assessment of their performance. If, like Foa, one was to read into this result a causal relationship from performance to familiarity, then one would expect that the *extreme* groups (i.e. the 'best' and the 'worst' workers) would be the most noticeable because of their performance, and that they would therefore be the ones with whom the foreman was best acquainted. This however is not the case. Instead, it was found:

> that the supervisor is well acquainted largely with the top workers and not-so-good workers, while the very poor and somewhat good workers are rather unknown to him.[108]

This asymmetrical pattern of distribution of the level of familiarity suggests that 'performance' is not the only factor which causes acquaintanceship and that, on the contrary, the level of familiarity influences the assessment of performance. One would assume that superior authorities are the people most able to make objective assessments, yet Slocum too points out the ambivalence of their judgements:

> In most organizations organized on a bureaucratic basis, promotions are supposed to be based on merit, but subjective elements such as personal preferences inevitably enter in to some extent. Personal relations skill may be fully as important as occupational competence in some organizations.[109]

The status criterion of 'educational standards' operates in a manner which shows different forms of the subtle restriction of central and peripheral role elements. I have already shown the structural limitations to the ability of employers to judge the functional qualifications acquired by employees in educational processes external to the work organization. Further, while educational institutions' assessments (as given in certificates of completion, diplomas etc.) could be used as the basis of an evaluation of individual qualification, they do not in fact make fine enough distinctions for use in recruitment and promotion decisions. Some diplomas etc. only confirm that the individual has a general occupational

---

[106] Cf. Caplow, *The sociology of work.*
[107] U. G. Foa, 'Types of formal leaders: their role perceptions and in-group contacts', *Transactions of the 2nd World Congress of Sociology* (London 1954), I, 110–14.
[108] *Ibid.,* 111.
[109] Cf. Slocum, *Occupational careers,* 241.

ability by a simple yes/no criterion, while in others the educational institutions restrict themselves to a scale of individual assessment that contains only a few grades. Such assessments show the groups with extreme qualifications as such, but produce a broad middle group which has no differences in qualification recognizable 'from outside'. If individual selection is to occur at all, then the recruiting authorities will have to fill in the resulting lacumae in information themselves, and this will necessarily involve symbolic substitutes which refer to peripheral role elements. The resulting contradiction is pointed out by Collins in his study of ethnic status differences:

> It is one of the shibboleths of modern management that advancement from job to job must be based on efficiency. By 'efficiency' is meant the capacity to do work. . . . Once, however, several candidates are admitted to possess the technical efficiency required for performance of the work [this is what education certificates confirm] other qualifications become important.[110]

Here once again we see the paradoxical process whereby the achievement principle is undermined by its own rigidly-sanctioned application: the very application of the achievement principle makes individual status and occupational destiny dependent on those (performance-irrelevant) qualifications which fit into a system of interests and cultural norms. Collins has researched the exceptional case of ascriptive status criteria which are based on the natural category of ethnic origin. Through participant observation of the processes of mobility within a factory, Collins showed how such ascriptive status criteria, as a 'pattern of ethnic job expectations, sponsorship and rejection',[111] are able to make the organizational hierarchy almost completely parallel with ethnic stratification:

> Whatever other considerations may have been involved in the promotion of employees, one of the key issues was always the ethnic identification of the individual proposed for promotion. Nationality or race was almost never explicitly declared to be a consideration in these situations but was always present. . . . Large areas of the plant hierarchy are almost completely occupied by members of one ethnic group.[112]

When ethnic origin was not already recognizable through such external characteristics as skin colour etc. (e.g. the difference between Irish and Polish immigrants), then the worker's name was used as an indicator of his ethnic origin—Collins noticed that some workers changed their family name to improve their prospects of advancement within the factory.[113]

[110] O. Collins, 'Ethnic behavior in industry', *AJS* 51 (1946), 293–8, here 293
[111] *Ibid.*
[112] *Ibid.*, 293, 295.
[113] This example shows an extreme form of how, under the pressure of desire for occupational mobility, 'identity' is adapted and subordinated to extrafunctional criteria.

All the same it was remarkable that even the groups which were discriminated against accepted mechanisms of ethnic status allocation as a matter of course, a fact which demonstrates the mutual stabilization of occupational and nationality roles:

> Since members of both management and labor have learned to recognize this system of ethnic job expectations and know fairly well how to adapt themselves to it, promotions are made year after year without, in the majority of cases, conflicts developing.[114]

Collins's study shows how functional qualifications, which by themselves do not enable an assessment to differentiate between individuals, are overlaid by a second level of ascriptive qualifications, and that these thus become important as an additional criterion for occupational status and mobility chances. Especially in the higher organizational ranks the opposite case should also be important: namely where an individual is promoted and allocated a status within the organization without yet having any of the functionally necessary qualifications, so status allocation is occurring through mechanisms of cooptation or protection on the basis of the individual's extrafunctional qualifications or loyalty. The attainment of the new status has to be legitimated by the *subsequent* acquisition of the functionally necessary qualifications. Once this has occurred, then certainly a relative coincidence of status and qualification is re-established; but considered generically, however, the mechanism of status change has been initiated by ascriptive or other peripheral role elements. Stone observed this type of promotion in the case of 'college training' courses, for which whitecollar workers are released from their jobs in order to acquire the skills they will need for a higher position. Since by definition the selection for such courses cannot be based in any way on the possession of the necessary qualifications for the higher positions, it must utilize other aspects of occupational behaviour. This process therefore involves

[114] Collins, 'Ethnic behavior in industry', 295.

C. Wright Mills quotes an excerpt from an interview in which a hospital administrator is questioned on the employment criteria applied to interns. The excerpt shows two things: first, in the employment of interns it is possible for ascriptive and ideological criteria not only to complement functional criteria but even to replace them; secondly, that for the organization the criteria that mattered for its personnel policy were precisely those on which the interns underwent a striking change of occupational role identity: 'One hospital administrator told ... how interns are selected: "The main qualification as far as I can see is 'personality'. Now that is an intangible sort of thing. It means partly the ability to mix well, to be humble to older doctors in the correct degree, and to be able to assume the proper degree of superiority towards the patient. Since all medical schools now have grade A there is no point in holding competitive examinations. ... Another reason for not holding competitive examinations for internships is that there are a lot of Jews in medicine." ' C. W. Mills, *White collar*, 12. Cf. also p. 63ff of this study.

the ascriptive allocation of the chance to acquire education and qualifications which can then be used to justify a higher status. It is thus through further education courses and similar arrangements that 'differential advantages which may exist on an informal level [are] legitimized and made part of official policy.'[115]

In this case social mobility inside the factory is being regulated by the distribution of training opportunities according to functionally peripheral characteristics of behaviour. Becker and Strauss describe the reverse case to this, where the chance to acquire knowledge relevant for promotion is only granted when the individual concerned is prepared to demonstrate loyalty to the interests and norms of the superior status group: if he does not do this, then he is denied all chances for training and hence for social mobility.

> Such systematic withholding of training may mean ... that an individual can qualify for promotion by performance only by shifting group loyalties.[116]

A similar mechanism lies behind the process whereby the departing member of an organization selects and 'works in' his successor.[117]

A study by Smigel[118] investigated the recruitment criteria applied in the employment of legally-trained personnel in the office of a large law firm. The study showed clearly that the great importance attached to a candidate's educational level does not relate primarily to the central elements of the work role, but rather to the prestige value of educational institutions and the cultural preselection which they carry out. The law firms which were studied

> want men who have pleasing personalities, are from the 'right' schools with 'right' social backgrounds, have a 'clearcut' appearance, and are endowed with tremendous stamina.

The firms compete with one another for the

> preferred lawyer—the personable man from one of the select Eastern law schools, who graduated with honors from an Ivy League college, and was at the top of his law school class.[119]

Such selection criteria have up to now been chiefly studied for the 'professions', and it is unclear whether they occur to the same extent in other status and occupational groups. Nonetheless, in the case of the lower ranks of employees, the effectiveness of ascriptive and other extrafunctional status criteria is well documented. There is a simple possible explanation for the fact that such criteria seem to play a special role in the 'professions' and also in the commercial

---

[115] Stone, 'Factory organization and vertical mobility', 30.
[116] Becker and Strauss, 'Careers, personality and adult socialization', 256–7.
[117] *Ibid.*
[118] E. O. Smigel, 'The impact of recruitment on the organization of the large law firm', *ASR* 25 (1960), 56–66.
[119] *Ibid.*, 57.

sector. In these areas there are two reference groups involved, both of which typically lack measures by which to make qualified and objective evaluation of functional qualifications, and who therefore have to rely on symbolic indicators of individual qualification. The two reference groups are on the one hand the customers, clients, patients etc. and on the other hand the superiors and co-workers. Both groups' symbolic assessments influence the success of the organization. This is the opposite to the case in relatively 'closed' organizations, which typically contain occupational tasks in which the interests of the organization can be safeguarded by only *one* authority, namely the superiors, controlling the peripheral elements of the occupational role. However, the success of such organizations as law firms, hospitals and commercial enterprises depends on whether the members of the organization (1) use the area of action and initiative at their disposal in line with the ruling interests, to which they must stand in a relationship therefore of functional loyalty, and *as well as this* on whether (2) they demonstrate to the other reference group (customers etc.) aspects of occupational behaviour which rank highly within the latter's (principally extra-functional) evaluative schema. Since the customers' and the superiors' extrafunctional evaluative criteria are not necessarily identical, this leads to an accumulation of non-achievement criteria. In the case of the law firm this would lead us to expect that (1) the Eastern law school as precondition for recruitment corresponds to the organization's interests in a particular ideological 'colouring' of occupational knowledge and that (2) discrimination against Jewish applicants is determined by the organization's concern to take account of its clients' antisemitic resentments and to thereby guard against the clients becoming irrevocably dissatisfied and no longer patronizing the firm. Since in comparatively closed organizations, such as administrative offices and production firms, the interaction partner in the subordinate position does not have the same amount of influence on the promotion of the organization's interests, the ascriptive status allocation mechanism does not occur to the same exaggerated extent as in commerce and in the 'professions'. These groups are therefore particularly well suited as subjects for research into extrafunctional definitions of occupational roles. We can see how obviously important the institutionally-maintained mechanisms of extrafunctional recruitment and promotion are if we investigate, from the point of view of business administration or the labour market, the *costs* which the operation of such criteria entails. These costs can be identified under three headings:

1   We have already pointed out that movements of upward mobility between positions with different work tasks (as is typical in organizations with a discontinuous qualification structure) entail

costs since such a change of position makes part of the occupational knowledge redundant and necessitates the acquisition of new knowledge. This sort of upward mobility therefore involves both the new costs of retraining individuals for their new jobs and the 'opportunity costs' of the now redundant training for their old jobs. In addition, promotion involves the prediction that the individual concerned is qualified for the new position, yet this prediction becomes less reliable the more advancement depends decisively on peripheral elements of occupational behaviour, for example on the demonstration of the *desire* for success. This has also been pointed out by Dalton in a study of intra-organizational mobility:

> Skills in pleasing appeared frequently to cause superiors not to see other qualities among aspirants and in some cases to appoint individuals who later failed to perform as expected.[120]

2   The same economic irrationality characterizes recruitment criteria which makes the admission to an occupational position dependent on peripheral role elements, either exclusively or in combination with central role elements. The application of extrafunctional and ascriptive measures always leads to a restriction of the supply of labour and thus to an increase in its cost. This is described by Smigel for the case of the recruitment of lawyers:

> The continuing restriction against Jewish lawyers cuts down the number of potential recruits who meet at least the high academic requirements demanded by large firms. . . . By eliminating some Jews from consideration the firms cut down their potential supply of academically superior individuals.[121]

These surplus extrafunctional elements of the institutionally-maintained occupational role definition have other results similar to the labour shortage which they cause. They establish a stereotype of the occupational role, a stereotype which affects the development of occupational aspirations and occupational choice.

> The range of diffusion of a public stereotype is crucial in determining the number and variety of young people from whom a particular occupation can recruit.[122]

3   Finally, in a certainly rather too perfectionist calculation, Roper has estimated the loss to the American economy as a result of ascriptive recruitment criteria at 13 thousand million dollars per year. These losses result from the ascriptive distribution pattern of unemployment[123] and from other deviations from the model of a

120 Dalton, 'Informal factors in career achievement', 414.
121 Smigel, 'The impact of recruitment . . .', 57.
122 Becker and Strauss, 'Careers, personality and adult socialization', 255.
123 Cf. also *The triple revolution: manifesto of the ad hoc committee on the triple revolution* (Santa Barbara 1964).

purely functional allocation of total social labour power.[124]

The fact that the losses caused by these types of dysfunctions and opportunity costs are tolerated to the extent that has been described provides a negative indication of the function served by ascriptive and other extrafunctional determinants of occupational status. It is obvious that these extrafunctional elements contribute to the stabilization of the organizational and cultural system of domination to an extent that makes acceptable the costs which they entail.

The required ideological 'colouring' of work in a particular occupation is seen as guaranteed not just by *education in particular institutions,* but also by membership of particular *nonwork* organizations. This results in an institutional linkage between occupational status and the roles held in other areas of life. In a group of managers (n = 226) studied by Dalton,[125] both determinants of occupational status were important. His study investigated the question 'by which means individuals rise to higher positions in organizations.'[126] Length of education proves to be the most important determinant of career success. However, a closer analysis of the data demonstrates how unimportant the acquired educational *knowledge* was for intra-organizational advancement:

> The data showed that only a minority of the managers were in positions relevant to their schooling, while at least 62 per cent were engaged in duties not relevant to their formal schooling. . . . For example, the industrial relations department was headed by officers with degrees in aeronautical and chemical engineering.[127]

The continued influence of the length of education despite such extreme differences between its content and the occupational function means that broad extrafunctional qualifications decisive for occupational mobility are acquired in the educational process. In the second part of his study Dalton focuses on the mechanism of 'institutional linkage' and shows how the following extrafunctional promotion criteria were decisive for management:

> (a) being a member of the Masonic Order, (b) not being a Roman Catholic, (c) having an ethnic background largely Anglo-Saxon and Germanic, (d) being a member of the local yacht club and (e) being affiliated with the Republican Party.

[124] Roper attempts to use survey material to produce a complete enumeration of the ascriptive mechanisms which play a role in personnel policy in industry. He lists discrimination according to skin colour, religion, sex, language, political attitude, nationality, social origin, property and education. E. Roper, 'Discrimination in industry: extravagant injustice', *Ind. and Lab. Rel. Rev.* 3 (1951–2), 584–9.
[125] Dalton, 'Informal factors in career achievement'; cf. also on the following Dalton, *Men who manage,* 161ff.
[126] Dalton, 'Informal factors in career achievement', 407.
[127] *Ibid.,* 408.

In Dalton's study the importance of the criteria declined in the order in which they are listed here.

The question of how such criteria operate is more important than that of their changing content. Here two interpretations are possible: loyalty is rewarded by promotion (1) at the level of relatively private sympathies, personal relationships and individual protection, or (2) through institutionalized mechanisms which are to a large extent independent of personal preferences and which contribute directly to the maintenance of power in the organization. From Dalton's study it is not possible to decide clearly between these two alternatives. While the second possibility is supported by the cooperative and relatively impersonal leadership style which distinguishes modern industrial administration from that typical of the small patriarchal firm, the validity of the first alternative is supported by the fact that the most influential criteria are derived from such relatively private areas of life such as religion and free time. This ambivalence shows that the claimed connection between extrafunctional selection principles and the need to maintain power in the organization must not be interpreted too directly. The mechanism of performance-independent status determination is oriented towards a dominant subcultural normative system, to the consolidation and reproduction of which it contributes. The mechanism does not only support economic and bureaucratic power, it also contains all-embracing prescriptions for the most diverse areas of life. The core of extrafunctional criteria, namely their contribution to the stability of domination, pervades all their other areas of influence.

In its negative aspect this mechanism perpetuates discrimination against cultural minorities. Forms of 'negative' ascription occur above all in the case of immigrants, refugees, foreign workers, ethnic and religious minorities etc. This form of repression is mediated through work, and its functional explanation lies primarily in the fact that the milieu from which these groups originate has equipped them with deviant orientations. In comparison to those groups who through primary socialization, school and occupational training have already acquired a more or less specific form of the industrial work ethic, these minorities are unable to the same extent to fulfil either the regulatory norms which make up an increasing part of the work role, or the 'surplus' extrafunctional definitions of the occupational role. The discrimination which these groups suffer is therefore explicable by the danger, deriving from their specific cultural 'equipment', that they would make inadequate or deviant use of the area of initiative the work role contains.

This argument leads to two hypotheses as to the characteristic type of position where minority groups suffering cultural discrimination will be over-represented. Firstly, we can assume that these groups will be located within the *lower* organizational status groups with little influence, since here their deviant orientations in occupational behaviour interfere less with the dominant system of interests and can damage it less than would be the case in the higher-status groups. Even if a deviant lifestyle is manifested in work in the lower ranks of the organization, it has there relatively little effect on the functional ability of the whole work system. The employment policy of public transport enterprises can perhaps serve as an illustration of this point: members of ethnic minorities are for example employed as bus or tram conductors, but not as drivers. Although both these positions allow relatively wide room for individual interpretation of the occupational role, autonomous action in the driver's role involves greater organizational risks than in that of the conductor.

However, our previous argument also yields a second hypothesis, namely that the mechanism of status ascription operates to place ethnic and cultural minorities disproportionately in the technologically and organizationally backward branches of production and services. In these areas a relatively 'nature near' technology permits strong initiatory influence on the work task, while at the same time the direct and personal relationships of domination and authority reduce the function of regulatory norms for the work process.

It is difficult to decide between these two hypotheses, since the two 'reserves' of cultural minorities partly coincide. It would be possible to demonstrate the combined effects of both mechanisms if it could be proved that cultural minorities are over-represented in the *lower* status groups of relatively 'nature near' services and production organizations. Unsystematic every day experience supports this assumption: in the Federal Republic of Germany the proportion of foreign workers employed is particularly high in the raw material, engineering and building sectors of industry, as well as in cleaning services for private households (cleaning women, laundries), local authority employment (city cleaning, rubbish removal etc.) and in the motor repair trade.[128]

A study by Nosow provides some reliable evidence of the link we have assumed between the culturally-defined division of labour, the technologically-determined requirements of work and the proportion of normative elements in the occupational role. Nosow investigated the operation of ascriptive and particularistic criteria of occupational distribution in a local labour market. His main finding agrees with our general hypothesis: cultural definitions determine the labour market processes more strongly than individual performance ability:

[128] It can be hypothesized that this technologically-determined pattern of ascriptive division of labour would remain even if the wage level and training period of the occupations were statistically controlled.

In all cases it was found that workers were concentrated as a group and that having particular skills did not determine the greater proportion of the particular type of workers within the given industry.[129]

A further result is revealing for our special concern, namely the sectors within which particular cultural minorities are concentrated. When total discrimination was broken down by economic sector— construction, transportation, services, the motor industry, forges and foundries, 'other manufacturing'—the forges and foundries were revealed as those most prepared to employ cultural minorities:

> Southern, Negro, and foreign born workers comprised 46·3 per cent of the workers in this industry while they were but 22·6 per cent of the total workers in the sample.[130]

Since work in forges and foundries clearly approaches closest to the 'nature near' type of work, this result can be interpreted as showing that this branch of industry is the least susceptible to deviant cultural orientations affecting behaviour at the work place, such that this is the branch which puts the least value on ascriptive recruitment criteria.

Sociological and sociocritical literature overwhelmingly treats the mechanisms which equip the occupational self-image with peripheral behavioural elements, and which ensure recruitment and promotion according to extrafunctional criteria, as deviations from the norm of a just and achievement-oriented pattern of social status distribution. This norm itself is seen as being in principle both legitimate and attainable, while its actual violation is explained through one of two models. Firstly, infringement is traced back to psychological mechanisms, as Inchheiser does with his assumption that individuals gain success for which their performance does not qualify them because they have machiavellian skills and an ability to get their own way, thus being able to avoid a 'just' assessment. The alternative model proceeds from a complex of ruling interests: this approach is taken by Dreyfuss[131] when he traces ideological differentiation in whitecollar hierarchies back to the intention of the capitalist class to split and discipline whitecollar workers, thus deflecting them from creating any class solidarity. Roper[132] follows the same argument—if in a weaker form—in a study which is typical of the intentions of many of the works cited here: he pleads for the correction of discriminatory organizational practices on the grounds that they lead to social conflict and losses for the economy. In both cases the yardstick for criticism and analysis is a univer-

[129] S. Nosow, 'Labor distribution and the normative system', in Nosow and Form, *Man, work and society*, 117–26.
[130] *Ibid.*, 119; p. > 0·001.
[131] Dreyfuss, 'Prestige grading'.
[132] Roper, 'Discrimination in industry'.

salistic, achievement-oriented model of social order,[133] a model which legitimates individuals' social status by classifying them exclusively according to their functional qualifications for work tasks. According to this unanimously-accepted model of social order, occupational position is measured by individual qualification, while social status is deduced from occupational position.[134]

By contrast, the purpose of the analysis that has just been made here was not to criticize *deviations* from the achievement principle by appealing to a normatively-maintained just order. Instead, the analysis aimed at challenging *the validity of this model of social order itself* by demonstrating its limits and its internal contradictions.

The subjective and objective mechanisms of status distribution that have been described here are not deviations from the achievement principle, explicable in terms of a psychology of interests; rather they are the results of the achievement principle's undiminished and institutionalized claim to validity. This claim comes up against work conditions that are technologically and organizationally determined, and in which more advanced forms of work make it impossible for the achievement principle to be applied. This discrepancy between the claims of the achievement principle and the conditions in which it applies transposes, as it were, its area of operation to the margin of the work and occupational role, especially since the preconditions for the fulfilment of those roles now involve normative orientations instead of being restricted to the category of technical rules. The transposed focus of the achievement principle leads to a change in its functions. In previous phases of industrial work the achievement principle at least had a critical sense, since it called for the rational allocation of individual productive power, even if this never became a full social reality. However, in the contemporary situation the achievement principle has become perverted and repressive. The way in which social status is distributed is now only a means of social control, rewarding the integration of the dominant interests and cultural values into the occupational role. In this way subcultural groups are classified and ranked according to standards of value which are beyond any public control. Those phenomena which have up to now been seen as violating the achievement principle are therefore in fact generated by the principle itself. If this is so, then it is no longer possible to criticize the discrimination and the behavioural controls which are imposed by extrafunctional occupational role definitions by appealing to the traditional model of distribution, one which legitimates differential life chances by proven individual qualifications.

[133] Cf. Parsons, *The social system*, 63–5.
[134] Cf. also Marx, 'Critique of the Gotha programme'.

Any possible alternative to this model of distribution would certainly have to include not just institutional mechanisms of recruitment and occupational mobility, but also the complementary level of subjective motives and aspirations: the acquisition and change of occupational roles would have to be based on other sets of motives than the individual receipt of advantages in relative status. However, contemporary technology now opens up perspectives which mean that it is no longer Utopian to postulate[135] that such motives could come into existence.

[135] Marx believed that the abstract egalitarian principle of a performance-dependent distribution of status could be abolished, but under the specific (and historical) condition that work itself was not 'abolished' but rather had 'become not only a means of life but life's prime want.' Marx, 'Critique of the Gotha programme', 19.

4

The achievement principle and labour income

The social status of the working individual is determined not only by his occupational position within a hierarchical organization, but also by the level of his wage or salary. These two dimensions of status—occupational position and income—are obviously not independent of one another, yet they are determined by different mechanisms. In addition, the dominant concept of society, the achievement principle itself, strongly emphasizes material rewards, so that for both these reasons a separate discussion of the income dimension is justified. This chapter will therefore first investigate the determinants of both the general wage level and the differences in wages between individuals and between positions, and secondly, the consequences for work behaviour of the predominant mechanisms of income distribution within organizations.

> In the conception of dependent work held in an economy based on exchange . . . the basic principle of performance plays for the first time a constitutive role in the wage structure. The hierarchy of social prestige has to be replaced by the hierarchy of achievement, in which achievement can be gauged on the one hand by market value and on the other by effective expenditure of effort, measured against a technical norm.[1]

However, it is in fact questionable whether this principle plays the role generally ascribed to it, given that a large amount of the income produced in industrial societies (outside the investment sector) is subject to *political* processes of distribution and redistribution, as well as to other mechanisms which also do not depend on performance. Thus, for example, in different economic sectors the same work receives a different level of wages because the different capital intensity in each branch affects the bargaining power of the two sides of industry, or because in one sector market conditions allow the employers to pass on wage increases to the consumers while in another they do not. Similar differences occur between individual firms and also between different regional labour markets.

In economic theory the basic explanation of income level is derived from the theory of marginal productivity. According to this, the in-

[1] Fürstenberg, *Probleme der Lohnstruktur*, 75.

come of all the factor units, including therefore that of the individual worker, is determined by the increase in value which each last factor unit adds to the total product. However, for several reasons this explanation has no operational value,[2] so that it is useless as an explanation of either the factual wage level or of the differences in wages between different work tasks. The theory may certainly be able to specify the upper *limit* of the wage *sum* of an entire firm or of an entire economy, but such information turns out to be trivial:

> As far as the shape of the wage structure is concerned, the explanatory value of marginal productivity theory—and hence of the concept of a clearly determined 'equilibrium wage'—must seem very low. Ultimately it reduces to the banal discovery that in the long term the employers cannot pay their employees more than the latters' work brings in.[3]

No economic theory is needed to discover the self-evident fact that the highest conceivable limit of wages is the productivity of labour (i.e. the maximum possible wage is when the firm's total income is turned into wages), while the lower limit is given by the worker's existence minimum.[4]

To demonstrate that the absolute level of wages is to a large extent independent of the results of performance (as measured by the market), it is instructive to look at the income distribution policies advocated by the participants in the wages conflict. Whenever the trade unions, the owners of capital, or state wages policies justify or criticize a given distribution of income, they all equally *abandon* the principle that the level of income has to be based on the individual or even the collective performance of the employees. Instead, the employees treat wages above all as the source of livelihood, and so are concerned with the real value of wages and not with the quantity or quality of work performance from which they derive. In this case the productivity aspect merely denotes an upper limit, beyond which wage claims are frequently seen as illegitimate.[5]

By contrast the employers and their organizations regard wages as a factor price, the level of which is fixed in collective agreements

[2] On the history of the theory of marginal productivity see W. Hofmann, *Einkommenstheorie* (Berlin 1965); for criticism see W. Krelle, 'Die Grenzproduktivitätstheorie des Lohnes', *Jahrbuch für Nationalökonomie und Statistik* 162 (1950); E. Preiser, 'Erkenntniswert und Grenzen der Grenzproduktivitätstheorie', *Schweizer Zeitschrift für Volkswirtschaft und Statistik* 89 (1955); Schumpeter, 'Das Grundprinzip der Verteilungstheorie'. In the explanation of income distribution, the theory of marginal productivity plays a role similar to that of functionalist stratification theory in the explanation of social status.

[3] Fürstenberg, *Probleme der Lohnstruktur*, 80.

[4] Cf. Hofmann, *Einkommenstheorie*, 242.

[5] Cf. R. Hoffmann, 'Produktivität als Fetisch: Gewerkschaftliche Motive einer indexgebundenen Lohnpolitik', *FH* 21 (1966), 765–73.

independently of the quantity and quality of the work performed: the wage contract then reflects the changing power constellation between the two sides of industry and also the conditions set by the current economic situation. Other important determinants of the wage level, such as bonuses and factory welfare payments, depend exclusively on the firm's employment policy and not on the value of labour. Finally, state social and economic policy has increasingly made into its basic principle the idea that the regulation of income distribution must be based more on needs which derive from collective support, and not on the claims which derive from achievement. This trend in the developement of the welfare state is underlined by the growing proportion of income recipients whose livelihood is based on state transfer payments, as well as by the tendencies in the USA towards a minimum wage guaranteed by the state.[6] In any case, as far as state income distribution and redistribution policy is concerned, it can be considered as proven that in every industrial society any attempt to make the absolute wage level dependent on categories of individual performance would lead to chaotic disruption of the whole economy.

The principle that increases in income should correspond to increases in productivity in the different sectors has also been partly sacrificed to the realization of the disruptive effects a blanket application of the achievement principle would have. Within and between the individual sectors of the economy productivity increases at different rates, so a wages policy which was based purely on productivity would not satisfy the need for an equal overall rise in mass purchasing power, yet this is a precondition for economic equilibrium:

> In a viable industrial society there are very narrow limits to the extent to which the earnings of broad groups of employees can remain behind the rising wages and salaries of the leading groups; the expansion of the production of goods depends upon rising mass purchasing power. . . . The real task is to harmonize the upward movement of wages in the individual sectors of the economy.[7]

In my opinion, this summary of the most important trends in income distribution policy necessarily leads to the conclusion that the evaluation of performance now plays a subordinate role in the determination of the *absolute* level of labour income. Instead, the wage level is subject to economic and political decisions which are unconnected to work and production at the individual workplace.

[6] This demand is contained in a document which marks the most advanced position in sociopolitical development in the USA—*The triple revolution: manifesto of the ad hoc committee on the triple revolution* (Santa Barbara 1964). The demand was put forward by the American trade union organization, the AFL-CIO, in connection with the debate on automation.

[7] B. Lutz, 'Hochmechanisierung und Lohnpolitik', *Atomzeitalter* 1 (1962), 21–2; cf. also Hoffmann, 'Produktivität als Fetisch.'

This makes all the more paradoxical the importance attributed to the achievement principle for the *relative* distribution of income. Factors such as the current state of the economy, monopolist influences on the collective labour contract and economic and social policy decisions all set up objective parameters for income distribution. These parameters can alter the real value of the individual's income just as much as decisions inside the firm as to the 'labour value' or the 'output value' of a particular work process. Nonetheless, in organizations the hierarchical differentiation of labour incomes tied to the fiction that real income, and all the life chances that go with it, is determined by the individual's qualifications and not by the overarching processes which reproduce the framework of economic and political domination.

In as much as the achievement principle claims to apply to the area of relative income differences, then there is a conflict between the individual (or position-specific) mechanisms of the distribution of labour income and the politicocollective ones.[8] At the same time it must not be forgotten that the distribution processes within the firm are in no way exclusively oriented de facto to the achievement principle. Over the last 50 years there has been a continuous growth both in welfare-type payments as a proportion of the total wage and in the extent of nonmonetary factory-level welfare measures.[9]

As the second chapter of this book argued, the legitimacy of distribution processes dependent on achievement is based on two complexes of arguments: first, the 'conditions of application' of the achievement principle (it must be possible to represent the different job functions on a single ordinal or even cardinal scale), secondly, the 'functions of the achievement principle' (those consequences considered to be beneficial which result from the application of the achievement principle to the distribution of status). Both groups of arguments can be interpreted directly as empirical assumptions and so are open to testing. If the assumptions can be disproved, this does not however directly challenge the achievement principle's claim to legitimacy—it would not be destroyed, but would merely have to be based on an alternative justification. However, given the institutionalized egalitarian pressures of the system, any attempt

[8] This opposition is conceptualized by Kosiol in the distinction between external and internal wage structures—the distinction between the wage problem of the factory and that of the national economy. Cf. E. Kosiol, *Leistungsgerechte Entlohnung* (Wiesbaden 1962), 7, 19.

[9] Cf. R. Reichwein, *Funktionswandlung der betrieblichen Sozialpolitik*(Cologne/s Opladen 1965). Kosiol also attempts to subsume these components of wages under the achievement principle, putting forward an interpretation which however is determined by clear ideological traditions: according to him, the so-called 'family wage' is also really a performance wage, 'in as far as it can be justified . . . by the contributions made to the improvement of the population pyramid.' Kosiol, *Leistungsgerechte Entlohnung*, 27.

to retain the existing structures of differential income distribution while basing them on new arguments would certainly be doomed to failure from the very beginning.

The achievement principle's claim to validity rests on certain empirical assumptions, and our attempt to test the most important of these will proceed by investigating the claim that the *relative level of labour income is determined by the differential value of individual or position-specific performance*. The norm bases its claim to authority on its alleged empirical consequences. However, instead of directly asking whether and to what extent the norm itself is fulfilled, we will ask whether the industrial sociological preconditions of the norm and of its claimed empirical consequences can in fact occur.

The achievement principle can only operate if a different value can be ascribed to different forms of work, and this in turn depends on whether they can be compared according to either input or output criteria. These categories in turn have to be broken down further: input into the differential costs of occupational training and the differential stresses of the work situation, output into physical, economic and functional concepts. As for the postulated empirical functions of the achievement principle, we will investigate here the most important, the incentive function. The following diagram shows the course of the discussion:

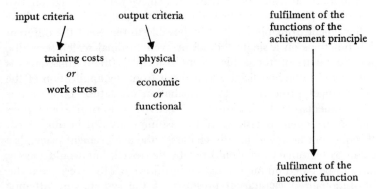

The principle of payment by performance: the differential value of work and performance provides the basis for the relative level of the labour income of positions and individuals.[10]

The achievement principle means that different concrete work tasks have to be reduced to a continuum which can define the differential value of the work involved in them, thus justifying the corresponding income differences. Whether in fact this is possible

---

[10] The arrows in the diagram indicate dependency.

depends primarily not on the elements which would be used to construct such a scale, but rather on the objective organizational and technological determinants of the work situation itself. The possibility of ranking roles then is not a question of arbitrarily defining a measure of comparison, but rather of the objective comparability of the contents of these roles themselves. The two most general criteria by which different work roles can be compared are (1) the productivity of the work (output criterion) and (2) the sacrifice, effort and strain which either is involved in either the work task itself or is a precondition for fulfilling the role (input criterion). Both criteria will first be investigated to see if they provide a valid measure for comparing typical work roles in industrial-bureaucratic organizations.

1   Labour productivity as a measure of comparison

In economic theory it is meaningful and customary to distinguish between 'physical' and 'economic' concepts of productivity. However, neither set of ideas yields a usable conceptual tool for differentiating and comparing work roles. According to the *economic* concept of productivity, the productivity, of a work role is only decided by the price which accrues to its results when they reach the market; but this price is subject to a multitude of market and power mechanisms which clearly cannot be seen as derived from the work role and how the individual carries it out. As far as the *physical* concept of productivity is concerned, the problem is that in only a small and diminishing number of work roles can the physical products produced be ascribed as distinct units to individuals. Further, using the physical idea of productivity leads to the problem of how to compare products that are qualitatively different. An additional difficulty makes both concepts of productivity unusable for our purpose of comparing work roles: in organized labour processes it is usually impossible to understand productivity as initiated and carried out by the occupants of individual work roles; rather it has to be seen instead as the activity of suprapersonal entities, consisting of both cooperative social relationships and technical forms of work.

These arguments leave us with only the criterion of *relative functional importance* as a possible way of evaluating comparatively the work roles of a hierarchical and cooperative work structure in terms of their productivity. Obviously, the problem that arises here is identical with the one posed at the macrosociological level by the functionalist theory of stratification—how can heterogeneous work functions be represented on a hierarchical continuum according to the single criterion of 'functional importance'? Even if we accept that for organizations functionality is one-dimensional, in that they have a single and explicit goal (something that cannot be assumed for whole systems), it is only possible to establish a clear hierarchical ranking of work roles according to the criterion of 'functional importance' or 'indispensability' to the extent that such a ranking is present within the structure of the organization itself.

However, our general model of organizational hierarchies means that we cannot simply assume that this precondition does actually exist. In the discontinuous type of qualification structure, the vertically-ranked positions are precisely *not* defined cumulatively along one central dimension of peformance—instead, the different positions involve quite different qualifications. To the extent that the organizational structure of the positions approximates a model in which the functional structure is divorced from the hierarchical division of labour,[11] the concept of the differential functional importance of position loses any obvious meaning: instead the organizational structure allows functions to be judged normatively or traditionally. As soon as the action and policy of the organization is determined by functional relationships of dependency, by delegation of special tasks and by functional differentiation, then every objective criterion of the differential functional importance of work roles for the organizational system simply evaporates.

Countless studies in the sociology of organizations confirm that as technological and organizational change continues in production and administration, these tendencies towards a discontinuous vertical distribution of tasks are becoming more prevalent.[12] Whenever superiority within the organizational hierarchy is no longer identical with functional superiority, then judgements of the differential

---

11 In the same way Bahrdt states that the 'work organization' and the 'leadership organization' have acquired a certain mutual independence, H. P. Bahrdt, 'Die Krise der Hierarchie im Wandel der Kooperationsformen'. *Proceedings of the 14th Congress of German Sociologists* (Stuttgart 1960), 105–6. At this stage of the study we now return to the subject of 'discontinuous qualification structure' discussed in the first chapter.

12 Cf. A. Gouldner, *Patterns of industrial bureaucracy* (Glencoe, Ill., 1954); idem, 'Organizational analysis', in R. K. Merton et al. (eds.), *Sociology today* (New York 1965), II, 400–428; H. P. Bahrdt, 'Fiktiver Zentralismus in Grossunternehmungen', *Kyklos* 9 (1956), 48ff.; idem, *Industriebürokratie*; idem, 'Die Krise der Hierarchie . . .'; D. Mechanic, 'Sources of power of lower participants in complex organizations', *Adm. Sc. Quart.* 7 (1962), 349–64; H. Hartmann, 'Bürokratische und voluntarische Dimensionen im organisierten Sozialgebilde', *Jb.f. Soz. Wiss* (1964), 111ff.: Hartmann characterizes this structural type of organization by the appearance in it of 'functional autonomy'. This is defined by the fact that 'the subordinates dispose of specialist knowledge and ability which is indispensable for the overall functioning of the organization.' He assumes that the trend is that 'in the course of growing specialization and differentiation it will become increasingly noticeable that in their own specialist area subordinates will in fact be superior to those in authority over them.' *Op. cit.*, 125–6; cf. also Hartmann, *Funktionale Autorität* (Stuttgart 1965), 102–21.

functional importance of work roles becomes arbitrary and random. Amongst others, Bates and Pellegrin[13] have recognized this weakness of the naïve notion of 'functional importance', and they therefore reject the attempt to validate it by using the criterion of indispensability. Instead, they try to find a more tenable criterion by defining functionally important occupational roles as follows:

> A position is functionally important to the extent that the role performances of persons in other positions are dependent on the role performance in that position . . . the responsibilities of the position are such that they can be performed correctly only by persons of exceptional training, experience and/or ability: and the function performed is highly valued by members of society and believed to be important.[14]

Yet, given the tendencies towards functional differentiation described by Hartmann, this rescue job has one obvious weakness—the key points of specialist competence cannot be simply identified with fixed positions and these then ranked as Bates and Pellegrin assume they can be, since the location of specialist competence changes from one work task to another. Bates and Pellegrin's argument then becomes circular when they judge the relative importance of occupational positions by the public assessment of those positions, and then proceed to explain this public assessment by how important the particular position is.

An apparently alternative argument entails the same sort of circularity. Once it is realized that the criterion of a work role's indispensability lacks any real content, the criterion of the replaceability of the role's occupant is used instead. However, obviously this replaceability is partly determined by price relationships in the market, and these in their turn would have to be explained by differential functional importance or be deduced from power mechanisms.

The conditions our argument assumes to apply in increasing areas of industrial and administrative work thus ensure that the output dimensions of work provide no way in which work roles can be differentiated in terms of their importance. The output dimension may at best enable separate individuals to be differentiated, but clearly only in cases where technological conditions allow individual variations in output, in other words only where there is scope for initiatory action. We will return to this point later in the study.

2 Work stress, amount of work and 'responsibility' as measures of comparison

Continuing the search for valid measures of comparison which

---

[13] Cf. H. Bates and H. J. Pellegrin, 'Congruity and incongruity of status attributes within occupations and work positions', *Soc. Forc.* 38 (1959–60), 23–8.

[14] *Ibid.*, 24.

H

would allow some statements of the relative 'value' of work functions, we now turn to the input dimension of work. Here it is easy to distinguish two large groups of characteristics in which differential input would have to be located: firstly, the stress and experience of effort which carrying out the work role involves, and secondly, the expenditure which the individual has to incur in training and in preparation for work.

We can begin with the category of expenditure on education. The discussion in the last chapter showed clearly that only a part (and probably at that a diminishing part) of the knowledge and ability gained in formal educational processes is directly functional for the fulfilment of concrete occupational work tasks. To the extent that this is so, it becomes meaningless to believe that all (i.e. including 'superfluous') expenditure on education is reimbursed by corresponding differentials in labour income.

In addition, it is noticeable that formal education processes are tending to expand in all industrial societies. This is shown both by the lengthening period of school education all citizens undergo and by the declining gap between the maximum and the minimum length of education. Obviously, in the socialist states of eastern Europe, with their systems of ten years in comprehensive schools followed by further education in technical schools, this trend is further advanced than in the West. Nonetheless, similar plans are becoming clear both in the USA and in western Europe. If, with all the necessary provisos, we can deduce from these signs a trend of a continuing increase in the average citizen's length of education, an extension above all of the lower educational streams and therefore a reduction in the relative differences between the worst and the best educated, then we can predict that the criterion of differential educational expenditure will lose its importance as a determinant of the differences in labour incomes. This also applies because, as we have seen, only a fraction of the results of education really benefit the work function, and the full level of occupational competence is only reached through learning processes which take place in the work itself.

Using statistical time series Muntz[15] has shown that since the beginning of the twentieth century the decline in the importance of educational level as a determinant of labour income has been reflected in a considerable reduction of differentials between occupational groups. Muntz's data is illuminating, even though he does not take into account changes in the structure of the demand for labour.[16]

[15] E. E. Muntz, 'The decline of wage differentials based on skill in the United States', *Int. Lab. Rev.* 71 (1955).
[16] Cf. W. Reder, 'The theory of occupational wage differentials', *Am. Ec. Rev.* 45 (1955).

Muntz starts from the assumption that the different wage rates for different labour functions can be partly explained by the corresponding differences in training costs, in particular from the 'opportunity costs' of training. According to this argument then, the cause of the decline in overall wage and salary differentials must be the fact that educational standards have both risen and become increasingly similar for all sections of the population.

| *Wage relationship between unskilled (= 100) and skilled workers, USA*[17] | | | | *Proportion of the corresponding age group attending high school* | |
| All industries | | Construction industry | | | |
Year	Skilled index	Year	Skilled index	Year	%
				1889–90	7
				1899–1900	11
1907	205	1907	185	1909–10	15
		1910	192		
		1915	199		
1918–19	175	1920	166	1919–20	32
		1925	181		
1931–32	180	1930	177	1929–30	51
		1935	179		
1937–40	165	1940	169	1939–40	75
1945–47	155	1945	154		
1952–53	137			1949–50	77

Since better educated workers are coming into the employment market in ever increasing numbers, while the proportion of uneducated workers is steadily declining, we have a situation where the potentialities of masses of individual workers are more evenly balanced than at any previous period in this industrial age. . . . The so-called 'unskilled' now tend to receive about as good an education as the 'skilled', make the same demands for a high standard of living, are probably equally adaptable to diverse industrial jobs and can be converted in most instances into skilled workers and technicians as the need arises. Here rests our fundamental explanation for the narrowing of wage differences.[18]

The existence of such a basic and socially created layer of general cultural abilities acquired through school makes invalid any form of 'input differentiation' of wages according to educational criteria.[19]

[17] *Ibid.*, 577–8. Data also partly from H. Obert, 'Occupational wage differentials', *Monthly Labor Review* 67 (1948), 130; see also, however, the results reported by P. C. Glick and H. P. Miller, 'Educational level and potential income', *ASR* 21 (1956), 307–12.
[18] Muntz, 'The decline of wage differentials . . .', 580.
[19] Baldamus also points out that the increase in in-job, non-formalizable training processes frequently reduces the cost of training borne by the individual to almost nothing. Cf. Baldamus, *Efficiency and effort*, 28ff.

According to Muntz however, precisely this development leads to
the creation of new forms of discrimination based on natural
categories, so that it cannot be expected that the wage structure
will become completely equalized:

> One cannot accept the premise that wage differentials will ever dis-
> appear completely. There are always some lower economic groups that
> will not receive a full wage, such as aged persons, some physically
> disabled workers, the mentally deficient and youths on first entering the
> industrial world.[20]

The achievement principle implies that expenditure on occupational training has both objectively and subjectively the character
of individual costs, and that these costs have therefore to be reimbursed to the individual. We now finally have to raise some doubts
as to the validity of this assumption. In all industrial societies the
traditional model, in which the individual financed his own education, is becoming atypical: it is being replaced by various forms of
socialization of the costs involved in education (examples of this
include the continuing extension of such methods of financing
education as government loans and scholarships). In addition, the
'opportunity costs' argument is also becoming less important: the
relative income forgone during the period of education (in relation
to the average earnings of people of the same age) is declining,
since the simultaneous increase and equalization of the length of
education ensures that only the groups in higher education (above
all in higher academic education) incur such losses of income. In
the controversy over the functionalist theory of stratification Tumin[21]
challenged the argument that education for the most highly qualified
occupations takes the form of a 'sacrifice'[22] which could later be
used to justify claims for a higher income:

> If one takes into account the earlier marriage of untrained persons, and
> the earlier acquisition of family dependants, it is highly dubious that
> the per capita income of the wage worker is significantly larger than
> that of the trainee.[23]

In addition to this diminished importance of opportunity costs,
Tumin introduces a further aspect which also questions the importance of the extra cost of above-average-length education:

> What tends to be completely overlooked ... are the psychic and spiritual
> rewards which are available to the elite trainees by comparison with
> their age peers in the labor force. ... There is ... the access to leisure

---

[20] Muntz, 'The decline of wage differentials . . .', 592.
[21] M. M. Tumin, 'Rewards and task orientation', *ASR* 20 (1955).
[22] This is one of the arguments of the functionalist stratification theory; cf.
Davis and Moore, 'Some principles of stratification'; Mayntz, 'Kritische
Bemerkungen zur funktionalistischen Schichtungstheorie', 10–28.
[23] Tumin, 'Rewards and task orientation', 56.

and freedom of a kind not likely to be experienced by the persons already at work.[24]

Together with the general trend towards the socialization of education and its costs, these compensations means it becomes ideological to justify differences in labour income by differences in the costs of education.

The same theory cannot be claimed to apply automatically to the stresses and effort which are immanent within the work process itself. Today, just as previously, there are workplaces in many sectors of industrial production which impose high physical costs on their occupants. Some workers have to put up with heat, dust, dirt and dampness; as previously, many work tasks make high demands as far as muscle and nerve strain are concerned, while from this aspect other jobs make almost no demands. It is in fact impossible to deny that there are large differences in stress between different workplaces.

All the same, there are clear signs that, in particular, progress in production technologies leads to an extensive reduction in the physical tiredness which the worker incurs in his work. This assumed trend can also be deduced from our general assumption that work is becoming less 'nature near', whereby the notion of distance from nature refers simultaneously to two facts: (1) measured in relation to the volume of all work processes, work with 'raw' natural materials relatively declines, and even where it still occurs in certain areas of the primary and secondary sectors it is increasingly mediated by technology; (2) closely related to this, there is a decline in the proportion of direct physical costs, in other words of the demands on 'raw' labour power. The main trends in the development of industrial and bureaucratic work lead us to expect that the subjective physical and psychic costs of work will both diminish and become increasingly similar in different workplaces. It follows that such costs will become increasingly inapplicable as a way of justifying wage differentials. The Marxist labour theory of value also includes the belief that the existence of different forms of labour implies differential reproduction costs of labour power—this idea too becomes increasingly irrelevant as technology continues to develop, bringing with it a reduction of work stress.

This conclusion is further supported by the argument developed in the first chapter, which claimed that there has been a change in the relationship between the technical and the normative elements of the work role. Work processes in which personal authority and supervisory relationships have been relaxed, and which depend on a type of action other than individual production, presuppose a high amount of regulatory normative control and an internalized

[24] *Ibid.*

goal orientation on the part of the workers. Therefore the share of normative orientations in the work role must increase: 'The most important labour problems of today are connected with the workers' motivation and not with his capacity.'[25]

One important difference between technical and normative rules is that the fulfilment of the latter does not entail *any subjective costs*, while rules of technical procedure are always linked directly to a subjective outlay. In fact, regulatory norms can be defined by the fact that obedience to them is not the result of any calculation of the costs and benefits involved: the losses and restrictions which eventually follow from obedience to regulatory norms are not consciously experienced as such.

When workers' motivation and identity are built into the functional conditions of work procedures, they create a productive force which is a social contribution to productivity, one created in primary and secondary socialization processes[26] which precede entry to the labour force. The organizations within which industrial and bureaucratic work takes place today are dependent on this productive force to a greater extent than ever before. Unlike physical and cognitive productive forces, this productive force entails no specific costs: the conditions necessary for its creation are identical with the cultural system itself. In addition to the already mentioned equalization of work effort, this growing relevance of the motivational elements of work behaviour is therefore a further factor which makes meaningless any justification of differential income on the grounds of the differential costs of labour.

Given that criteria of both productivity and of effort are becoming vague in the way we have already described, the validity of any relative evaluation of work functions becomes rather questionable. In addition, classification of tasks in terms of their productivity and of the demands they make on the worker are already dubious, yet where new work technologies are introduced this frequently leads to these classifications being changed not in parallel but rather in opposite directions—typically, technological improvements increase the physical productivity of a job and at the same time reduce the effort the work involves:

> with better methods of production, worker efficiency (output per unit of time) may increase while effort remains the same or decreases.[27]

An objectivist method of estimating the value of work thus leads to conflicting results, depending on whether it emphasizes the input or the output side of the work task. This discrepancy means that

[25] W. Baldamus, 'Type of work and motivation', *BJS* 2 (1951), 44–58, here 58.
[26] Cf. Baldamus, *Efficiency and effort*, 83–5.
[27] H. Behrend, 'The effort bargain', *Ind. and Lab. Rel. Rev.* 10 (1957), 512.

there is no valid base for the way in which organizations reclassify work positions which are affected by technological change. In fact, this dilemma is normally resolved by traditionalistically retaining a hierarchy of sanctioned claims, a hierarchy which is now no longer based on any form of functional criteria:

> Many factors consider it necessary to ensure a continuity in the wage structure despite technical changes. . . . In general the principle is to retain rights that have already been acquired, i.e. when technical progress reduces the value of a work position, for some time at least the workers retain their previous basic wages. On occasions this can lead to large differences in earnings at one and the same work place, if it includes both workers with a higher basic wage inherited from the old section together with new recruits who at once receive a lower basic wage corresponding to the new working conditions.[28]

E. Jacques[29] uses the idea of responsibility in his search for a method of concretizing the achievement principle, such that a valid comparison can be made of heterogeneous work functions. According to Jacques, *differential responsibility* forms the basis of the status hierarchy of industrial work organizations. Jacques' argument seems to aim at justifying the achievement principle:

> It is of special importance to have a yardstick for measuring level of work, because of the widespread endorsement of the principle that payment should be directly related to the level of work done.[30]

A comparison of the jobs at all levels of the hierarchy of an English engineering firm showed that they could be represented on a continuum[31] based on the length of the action cycles specific to each position: the higher the position in the hierarchy, the longer the time horizons and the feedback periods.[32] Jacques recommends that the wage differences between jobs should be based on this time criterion:

> When level of work is measured by time-span . . . an equitable work-payment-structure can be found: payment that is consistent with this

[28] Ifo-Institut für Wirtschaftsforschung, *Soziale Auswirkungen des technischen Fortschritts* (Berlin/Munich 1962), 68–9; here we can merely point out that this violates the principle that work and payment should be equivalent. Cf. also H. Heitbaum, 'Lohnermittlung bei fortschreitender Rationalisierung und Automation', *WWI-Mitteilungen* 9 (1956); W. Schaefer, 'Lohnpolitik und Lohntechnik', *GMh* 5 (1954); E. Jacques, *Measurement of responsibility: a study of work payment and individual capacity* (London 1956), 9–10.
[29] Jacques, *Measurement of responsibility*.
[30] *Ibid.*, 5.
[31] This is incidentally challenged by an American follow-up study which uses the same categories as Jacques but far more precise research techniques. See P. S. Goodman, 'An empirical examination of Elliott Jacques' concept of time span', *Hum. Rel.* 20 (1967), 155–80.
[32] Jacques, *Measurement of responsibility*, 24–5.

structure will be found satisfying by members fully established in jobs; work will be done in a relatively efficient, competitive, and decisive manner ...; and there will be freedom from grievances about differentials between members and between group or grades of members.[33]

Obviously this dimension of ability according to 'time-span-capacity'[34] derives from the paradigm of the employer's capital investment:

Work may be described as a kind of investment behaviour—investment in one's foresight, one's ability to foresee consequences of one's actions.[35]

However, it is also clear that long-term planning is not functional for all work tasks. Ability to plan ahead is really a qualification which is largely demanded for management positions, and it is primarily there that it can actually be used, since under the conditions of capitalist production management has a monopoly of long-term planning. It follows that to construct an income hierarchy in the way Jacques proposes is to produce an almost tautological measure of wage status in relation to management work tasks. In that this interpretation of the achievement principle focuses on the role contents of dominant groups and positions,[36] it entails an unexplained and unjustified acceptance of the status quo. In any case, this model cannot in any way challenge the thesis that for broad and indeed expanding areas of the organizational system of the division of labour, no valid criterion for the differential evaluation of positions can be derived from the individual work task.

3   The normative basis of income distribution

Clearly, then, there are insuperable difficulties involved in any attempt to develop a hierarchy of the value of work functions by using the technical elements of the work role. Therefore, we have to ask what factors are really responsible for the income hierarchies which do exist, and which cannot be explained by market or power processes. Here almost all the relevant studies agree, basing their

[33] *Ibid.*, 85.
[34] *Ibid.*, 90.
[35] *Ibid.*, 92.
[36] The role characteristics of management positions correspond with the cultural characteristics of the strata from which managers typically are recruited: Jacques' concept of 'time-span-capacity' is almost identical to the 'deferred gratification pattern' which Schneider and Dornbusch have have shown to be a distinguishing characteristic of the middle class. Seen in this way, the concept of 'time-span capacity' loses its instrumental character of a specific ability for production, and instead has to be understood as one of the forms of cultural 'equipment' which turn out to be positively functional in specific positions. Cf. Schneider and Dornbusch, 'The deferred gratification pattern: a preliminary study', *ASR* 18 (1953), 142–8.

answer on the existence of a *consensus* over the relative value of work functions, a consensus which is firmly institutionalized but also completely independent of technical elements. This consensus cannot be explained by input and output criteria, even though it can be rationalized by using productivity dimensions in an ideological manner. The argument is summarized by Livernash:

> Ratings do not employ measuring rods which can be validated to any meaningful degree apart from group judgement. No physiological measurement of fatigue would validate the physical effort ratings; statistical records of damaged product would not validate responsibility ratings, training time records would not distinguish between required, desired and actual experience. . . . Agreement is the essence of the detailed placement of jobs and of the formulation of the skeleton.[37]

Thus technical criteria are too vague to determine wage status, while their application becomes more and more problematical as those trends in industrial work develop which we have already described. As a result a given set of wage differentials becomes solely based on a consensus that the wage differentials are justified, while the main carriers of this consensus are the employees themselves: workers attempt to legitimate the relative size of their own and others' wage claims by using normative traditions which define their wage status as 'suitable', 'correct', 'just' etc. This consensus has to be shared by the occupants of those positions which determine the distribution of income, as well as by the trade unions and also by wide sections of the general public. This in a certain sense arbitrary mechanism, shaped by the scales of value which the whole society accepts, is strongly emphasized by Baldamus.[38] According to him, while the total income available to labour is determined by market and power processes, its relative distribution has to be explained by an irreducible system of normative aspirations:

> Neither economic theory nor common sense provides a simple and sufficiently general answer as to how the relative shares of the contributions to the product are determined, e.g. why different amounts of wages go to skilled and unskilled work, to manual and non-manual effort, to direct and indirect labour. . . . The imputation of wages to different kinds of labour is open to ethical judgements . . . : all the popular arguments over wage-differentials can always be reduced to questions of 'fair', 'equitable', 'reasonable' or 'proper' shares in the joint result of occupational activities. The problem of justice in the distribution of such shares is necessarily a social one.[39]

It is in line with this thesis that when there is a question of

---

[37] E. R. Livernash, 'Wage administration and production standards', in A. *Kornhauser et al.* (eds.), *Industrial conflict* (New York 1954), 330–44, here 336–7.
[38] Cf. Baldamus, *Efficiency and effort* and *Der gerechte Lohn* (Berlin 1960).
[39] Baldamus, *Efficiency and effort,* 26.

improving the relative income status of any one occupational group, it is noticeable that an appeal is frequently made to general social values and to professional skills as a justification for the claim. From our point of view, what is really important here is that in the final analysis the existing system of wage differentials is only maintained by the workers' own culturally determined motives, aspirations and 'standards of suitability'. Both through pre-job socialization and at the workplace itself, the workers acquire a definition of their role which contains norms specifying how much of the effort involved in the particular job should be reimbursed. This standard of what is a suitable compensation is not based on any objective technical or physiological criteria, so as a result it can only very inadequately be translated into the language these criteria entail:

> Theoretically at least we can assume that such definitions of what is suitable or reasonable are more important than the actual amount of effort.[40]

In other words, the system of wage grades within a firm rests upon a normative basis.

This situation introduces one extrafunctional element of the work role, in that workers themselves accept the wage level applicable to their particular jobs. If the economic relationships of domination are to be maintained, then the organizational system within which the division of labour occurs has to ensure that it is not just the threat of dismissal which makes the workers accept the going market price for their labour: under welfare state conditions, this *particular* control mechanism is inadequate, since not only can it be manipulated by collective bargaining, but also, and most importantly, it can simply be rendered inoperable by conflict within the firm (go-slows, accidents, wild strikes, illness etc.). Therefore, if modern work organizations are to function, one precondition is that the workers should have a high level of *manifest satisfaction* with the wage offered, both absolutely and in relation to other wages. However, this normatively-mediated readiness on the part of the workers to orient themselves to, and then accept, a particular relative wage status has nothing to do with the work function itself. The entire system of status and domination within modern industrial social organizations depends upon the fact that 'most workers most of the time accept the rate as a traditional and customary part of the job.'[41] Trends in technology, social policy and organization all work together towards a situation in which wage satisfaction is becoming a permanent sine qua non for modern industrial organizations. Baldamus explains this situation by pointing out the growing

40 Baldamus, *Der gerechte Lohn*, 64.
41 Livernash, 'Wage administration and production standards', 334.

sensitivity of work organizations to their members' experience of constraint and strain, in so far as this is not compensated for by a 'suitable' wage.

> The intensity of strain remained a subjective experience which could not materially affect the level of sustained performance so long as the coercive pressure to work was fully intact. With coercion reduced by conditions inherent in the Welfare State, variations of strain in different situations can now be expressed in overt conduct.[42]

The fact that the system of wage differentials rests on a normative basis has a further consequence. The inadequacy of personal authority and of the negative sanctions of the labour market increase the employees' influence on their own standards of what is a 'suitable' payment. At the same time however, if a situation of relatively stable wage satisfaction is attained, then this equilibrium is equivalent to a much more thorough integration of the employees into the organizational structure than was ever possible before under conditions in which 'the intensity of strain remained a subjective experience.' If, on the one hand, the different groups of employees can more easily get their almost caste-like wage aspirations satisfied, this means on the other hand that large areas of motivation are now tied to the current status quo of power and income distribution. While the different aspirations of the different occupational groups can and must be granted, the very fact that this does occur blunts the experience of conflict and reduces the ability to articulate it. Wage differentials thus acquire the character of a confirmation, independent of performance, of the positional groups' self-evaluation. Wage differentials are therefore also a means whereby the management can discipline employees by the differential distribution of rewards.

Baldamus has attempted to base an outline theory of exploitation on the fact that both the regulatory norms of occupational activity and specific wage aspirations derive from a pre-existing cultural base, transmitted through socialization processes. According to Baldamus, the labour power available to a society is quantitatively determined and even 'produced' by the dominant system of cultural norms. The duty to work and an ethic of work are the 'institutional (non-economic) factors which underpin the worker's motivation in a capitalist system.'[43]

> In the final analysis, it is the moral obligation to work which explains the distribution of the labour product in the employer's favour. The society's moral capital, the customary pressure to work, flows to the employer as his private property.[44]

This applies not only to the wage quota, it also determines the

---

[42] Baldamus, 'Type of work and motivation', 57.
[43] *Ibid.*, 56.
[44] Baldamus, *Der gerechte Lohn*, 59.

extent and type of the existing wage differentials, the latter being based on the differing and culturally-defined income aspirations of work functions and occupations, since wage differentials tend to be only justifiable to the extent that their validity is rooted in the norms and attitudes of the workers. Wage differentials certainly do appear to have some validity, but this is only because the *fiction* of their technical justifiability has itself been elevated into a normative tradition. Precisely because under the technological conditions of advanced societies the rational basis of this tradition has dwindled down to a few and dubious remnants, the normative tradition itself has to be buttressed with an extreme degree of institutionalized support. In other words, if the consequences were drawn from this development and the traditional achievement-based interpretation of status differences accordingly rejected, then the whole way in which social relationships of status and domination are legitimated would collapse.

4   Work study and performance evaluation techniques

The fiction that the differential value of work and performance can be objectively measured is made part of the practice of organizations by a series of techniques, of which the two most important are analytical work study and time-and-motion study. The individual form of these two techniques and the different methods they involve cannot be discussed in more detail here. However, they both have in common the belief that it is possible to find criteria for ascertaining the relative value of an average performance at one workplace (the 'job value'), or that 'normal times' for work can be determined by purely technical methods: whether or not these norms are fulfilled thus provides a means of differentiating wages according to the 'productivity value' of the individual's work.[45] The job value is

> the symbol for the sum of the demands placed on the worker carrying out particular work at a particular workplace at 'normal human performance'.[46]

Thus, according to work study theory, as soon as a wage level (the 'basic') is fixed for only one job, then in principle an objective wage scale can be worked out for all the other work functions:

> Between the value of the job and the value of the wage there exists a

[45] Cf. H. Euler and H. Stevens, *Die analytische Arbeitsbewertung als Hilfsmittel zur Bestimmung der Arbeitsschwierigkeit* (Düsseldorf 1952); E. Kosiol, *Leistungsgerechte Entlohnung*; H. Heitbaum, 'Vom Arbeitswert zum Lohn', *GMh* 6 (1955); H. W. Hetzler, *Die Bewertung von Bürotätigkeiten: Grundlagen und Verfahren* (Cologne/Opladen 1961).
[46] Heitbaum, 'Vom Arbeitswert zum Lohn', 90.

relationship of a form such that a wage value can be calculated for every job value.[47]

In general calculating job values means considering four groups of requirements made on the worker: these have to be located and measured for every work role. These factors or 'requirement areas' are:

1 specialist knowledge
2 strain
3 responsibility
4 work, conditions and environmental influences.

Obviously, these dimensions of performances are categories which refer to the 'input' to work and most of them (i.e. points 1, 2 and 4) have already been discussed. This discussion came to the conclusion that the dominant trends in the development of industrial work make it likely that these requirements will become increasingly similar in different positions, making obsolete the idea that work functions have different values.

However, this general thesis has to be supplemented as far as the third factor (responsibility) is concerned. At least in West Germany, job-evaluation procedures see 'responsibility' differently to Jacques' interpretation of it as 'time-span-capacity'. Thus Hetzler defines it as:

> The amount of responsibility is greater, the more damage that can result from unreliability, negligence or carelessness on the part of the worker.[48]

It is even less valid to subsume this sort of definition of responsibility under the category of expenditure on work than is the case with Jacques' definition, which itself is already more a measure of the cultural attitude of deferred gratification than of any form of subjective strain. The idea of responsibility current in West German job evaluation makes the occupants of positions responsible for risks of which the frequency and economic extent are determined by the structure of the organization, while the definition does not even claim any logical link with the category of work effort. If one qualification for a job is exercising a certain amount of care, since this is a quality that is culturally transmitted, it is an element of work that has no 'costs'. Quite apart from this, it is impossible to measure the extent of the consequences which have been *avoided* because the worker has been careful. Where care only means paying attention, preventing a thousand pounds' worth of damage needs no more effort than is needed to prevent only one pound's worth. To this extent the concept of responsibility is thus an extraneous

[47] *Ibid.*
[48] Hetzler, *Die Bewertung von Bürotätigkeit*, 38.

element in the list of the four dimensions of job evaluation. There are also arguments which would suggest that in industrial organizations even this 'requirement type' is becoming less important as a way of making distinctions within the system of work positions: owing to growing capital intensity and growing functional differentiation, the possible economic consequences of errors increase at every position, while at the same time they become more equal between the different positions. In one study of automation Faunce points out:

> In such a situation [automation] the position of each worker becomes more strategic both in terms of his ability to stop production and in terms of his increased responsibility stemming partly from the increase in machinery investment per worker.[49]

Thus the very dimensions which job-evaluation procedure uses do not coincide with the reality of work in technologically-advanced industrial organizations: the objective reduction of the differences in labour input increasingly removes the basis of any application of the types of requirements that have been discussed here.

In addition to this, *aggregating* and weighting the individual dimensions of strain into a unitary 'index of value' is a problem which can only be resolved completely arbitrarily. Despite all their apparent exactness, job evaluation procedures do nothing towards solving this problem: Heitbaum is therefore being quite logical when he makes weighting something which should be decided by the collective wage contract.[50] The problem of weighting can only be avoided when the different positions of an organizational hierarchy change on their separate dimensions in the same direction and in the same proportion: in other words the superior position B would have to have higher requirements than position A equally in terms of ability, responsibility and environmental influences. Quite clearly, the 'discontinuous qualification structure' which distinguishes the large industrial firm from a craft-type organization makes any such assumption illusory. For this reason, job evaluation has no option but to create indices which include cultural definitions of the prestige of the different types of requirements. As a result, despite the impressive use of apparently objective measurement procedures, analytic job evaluation has to fall back on the normative substructure—the institutionalized value hierarchies which these very procedures disguise.

One other brief point has to be made about procedures for assessing *individual* differences in performance and corresponding wage differentials. Unlike job evaluation, which is based on largely

---

[49] W. A. Faunce, 'Automation in the automobile industry: some consequences for in-plant social structure', *ASR* 23 (1958), 401–7, here 407; similarly, Fürstenberg, *Probleme der Lohnstruktur*, 64.
[50] Cf. Heitbaum, 'Vom Arbeitswert zum Lohn', 92.

fictitious criteria of *job requirements*, evaluating individual differences in work behaviour *within* one position (i.e. at the same workplace) focuses on the productivity of the individual. Here work study is used first of all to specify normal times or normal production per time unit, and then different methods of piecework or bonus payment are used to reward higher productivity with differential wages. How effective such methods of individual productivity assessment and payment actually are as 'incentives' is a question to which we will return later. At the moment we merely have to see that there is a series of restrictions on whether these methods can be actually applied. Firstly, as the proportion of regulatory norms in the occupational role increases, it is becoming increasingly impossible to specify the value of individual performance. Dimensions of 'performance' such as 'honesty, personal integrity, loyalty to the firm, professional behaviour, orderliness, punctuality'[51] are in reality not technical rules for carrying out the job but rather the normative preconditions for doing so. They cannot therefore be fitted into a grading system, but have to be judged instead in dichotomous terms. This is a point which is also conceded by Hetzler:

> A whole series of personality characteristics are completely ruled out because they cannot be graded: a worker is either honest or punctual or is not. This either/or alternative means that these characteristics can provide no graduated categories and these are a precondition for measuring job values.[52]

Individual differences in performance can only be demonstrated within the area of freedom allowed by initiatory influence, so the extent of this form of influence would itself have to be investigated. In the case of a steelworks,[53] Lutz and Willener have shown that the extent of initiatory influence decreases as the level of mechanization rises. This change in the form of influence can be taken as a general characteristic of the development towards automation:

> The primary function of the worker in automated industries changes from that of operating the machine and checking its performance to that of responsibility for skilled maintenance of a self-operating, self-regulating, integrated machine process. . . . The general wage structure and methods of payment are bound to be affected by automation. The use of incentive systems such as piece rates . . . is no longer feasible when production is reduced to a continuous flow process in automated industries.[54]

[51] Hetzler, *Die Bewertung von Bürotätigkeit*, 44.
[52] *Ibid.*, 45.
[53] Cf. Lutz and Willener, *Mechanisierungsgrad und Entlohnungsform*.
[54] W. A. Faunce and H. L. Sheppard, 'Automation: some consequences for industrial relations', *Transactions of the 3rd Congress of Sociology* (London 1957), II, 165ff., here 167; cf. also G. Friedrichs (ed.), *Automation–Risiko und Chance* II (Frankfurt a.M. 1965).

The way wage forms have developed also shows clearly that as mechanization takes on more advanced forms it becomes impossible to locate the results of any one individual's work in isolation. In many cases individual piecerate systems, in which the individuals' wages rise in proportion to their output, are replaced by group piecerate systems, in which wages increase less than proportionately to output.[55] The final development is collective bonus systems, based on data external to the firm (such as turnover and profits) and therefore abandoning completely any attempt to reward the functional contribution of the individual worker to the firm's goal:

> More and more today incentive plans for the whole factory are preferred to systems which are geared to the individual worker [since] the ever greater prevalence of team work makes it difficult if not impossible to calculate the exact performance of the individual worker.[56]

In other and less mechanized work situations the extent of initiatory influence is vague, varying from day to day and from job to job. Since here the worker cannot control the changing external conditions of the work situation (which determine how much initiatory influence he can exercise), any comparison of individual performance becomes meaningless. As in the case of the concept of responsibility, this situation ensures that the objective work conditions and changes in them are taken to be the individual workers' performance, for which the workers are then praised or blamed accordingly. This point is made by Brayfield and Crockett in a discussion of research techniques:

> To be valid, a comparison of output between two individuals must equate the conditions under which the individuals operate.
>
> However, one salesman's territory may be potentially more fruitful than another's. . . . Two machines may vary in their potential output, in their state of repair, and in many other ways. Frequently, there are, in addition, external restraints on productivity. Output in a factory may be determined by the speed of the assembly line or the speed of the machine, by the amount of materials provided to an individual by some feeder line, or by the quality of the material being processed. Variation in situational factors such as these will affect total productivity no matter what the level of individual job performance.[57]

Under such conditions, manifest differences in output may appear to confirm the idea that differences in individual ability exist, yet basically this 'confirmation' is based on obscuring the difference

[55] Cf. Lutz and Willener, *Mechanisierungsgrad und Entlohnungsform*.
[56] F. Fürstenberg, 'Die Soziale Funktion von Leistungsanreizen im Industriebetrieb', in P. Attelander (ed.), *Konflikt und Kooperation im Industriebetrieb* (Cologne/Opladen 1959).
[57] A. H. Brayfield and W. H. Crockett, 'Employee attitudes and employee performance', *Psych. Bull.* 52 (1955), 396–428, here 410.

between the individual's ability to work and the technological and organizational conditions under which he works.

Certainly, it cannot be denied that in the long term there will always be a few workplaces where there will be a clear opportunity of exercising initiatory influence. However, in her anlysis of the working of productivity payment systems, S. Shimmin[58] has pointed out that, even at such workplaces, differentiating wages according to the amount of individual output leads to dubious results. It becomes pointless to differentiate individual wages not just when initatory influence is low, but also when it is high—i.e. when the workers can achieve an increased quantity of production by reducing the quality and/or increasing the usage and wastage of materials. Shimmin's study shows that management has reservations about large differences between individual wages:

> Instances were given of increased wastage of materials and of larger quantities of spoilt work following the introduction of a wage incentive scheme. . . . In the view [of supervisors], the problem [was] the tendency for quantity to be produced at the expense of quality.[59]

There turns out then to be only a relatively small area in which the structure of the work situation makes it at all possible and meaningful for wages to take into account the value of individual performance: as mechanization of industrial production and administrative work continues, this area diminishes further. The next section of this chapter will consider the extent to which, in this remaining area, the assumed allocative and incentive functions of the achievement principle are in fact effective.

After this critique, limited to a few theses, of the 'objective' procedures of job and performance evaluation, we now have to put these interpretations of wage differentials into a broader context. We have seen that neither input nor output categories can be used to create a valid way of relating the jobs in industrial organizations to each other in terms of their value. Instead, the existing system of wage relationships is based on a hierarchy of position-specific claims, sanctioned by a relatively stable consensus amongst the participants. This consensus itself is stabilized by the fiction that the hierarchy of wages and authority can be technically justified. In reality, however, this hierarchy tends to be based exclusively on cultural definitions stating which claims to status can be legitimately linked to which work functions. The distribution pattern of occupational prestige is completely independent of the changing characteristics of the work roles, but it is nonetheless astonishingly

[58] Cf. S. Shimmin, *Payment by results* (London 1959).
[59] *Ibid.*, 67, 134; cf. also the discussion of the dysfunctional results of the application of simple, multiple and composite criteria of success in V. F. Ridgeway, 'Dysfunctional consequences of performance measurements', in Hill and Evans (eds.), *Readings in organization theory* (Boston 1967).

I

permanent.[60] This makes it probable that a similar scale exists which provides a normatively defined ranking of the different income and lifestyle claims for the holders of the different occupational functions.

The cultural conditions which define status thus have a 'technical' pseudo-justification, and this is obviously functional in maintaining the legitimacy of an overall social system which is characterized by massive inequalities of power and income. The 'technical' justification of status by performance forms the most general model of legitimacy, not just for organizational hierarchies but analogously also for wide areas of the social class and social stratification system. In this situation a major system problem emerges: how can the system of status distribution be legitimized with categories deriving from 'objective' technical rationality, when the system is both dominated by cultural traditions and is at the same time no longer justifiable in terms of these traditions.

This legitimation problem provides a way of interpreting job and performance evaluation methods. Despite their scientistic procedures, they provide no way of 'objectively' ascertaining status relationships. On the contrary, they are one of the most important ways in which the system of status distribution, supported by the dominant norms and interests, is technically mystified and justified. In contradiction to its own self-understanding, job evaluation does *not* have the function of explaining or even correcting this system, but instead its function is merely to confirm the status quo by means of 'objective' measurement procedures. Precisely because its indexing is so arbitrary and its 'requirements' dimension so inadequate, it can be covertly adapted to the ruling norms of income distribution.[61] Baldamus judges performance evaluation practice in the same way:

> The true purpose of scientific objectivity in the practice of work measurement is precisely the opposite of what it claims to be in theory . . . precision and consistency of technical terms and measuring appliances . . . have the functions, not of eliminating the intrusion of effort conceptions, but, on the contrary, of detecting and making them all the more amenable to consistent guesswork. The true purpose of time-study, in other words, is to guess as consistently as possible the purely subjective element of effort standards, and subsequently, to adjust rates of pay in accordance with them.[62]

From time to time the theoreticians of job evaluation come up against the ideological limits on their own self-understanding; but all the same, these limits remain undisturbed in the faith that sometime in the future the problems will be resolved merely by further refining the procedures:

[60] Cf. the discussion of the study by Kriesberg in chapter 3 above.
[61] Ifo-Institut für Wirtschaftsforschung, *Soziale Auswirkungen* . . ., 67.
[62] Baldamus, *Efficiency and effort*, 45–6.

For the time being it is not possible to locate the valence [of work functions] with the help of the relevant scientific procedures, and therefore the only way in which the correctness of the valence can be assessed is ... by proof in practice.[63]

In other words, in the final instance the validity of a 'work valence' depends upon whether it corresponds to the culturally-sanctioned income claims of a group of workers.

We can now summarize this section. Despite their objectivist appearance, the *work values* determined by analytic job evaluation are nothing but the expression of culturally-sanctioned status claims. In the same way, performance norms which provide the basis for the determination of individual *performance values* do not express any objective normal results (in the sense of a physiology of work) of a work activity, but merely reflect group-specific norms of what is a 'suitable' work result. Behrend has therefore defined a 'system of beliefs' as the basis of individual wage differentials.[64] In the final analysis there is a normative basis to both work values and performance values. This is mystified but not altered by the fact that the scientistic measuring operations of work study express these norms as merely technical quantities. This linkage can be presented schematically as follows:

	Measurement object	*Measurement dimension*	*Normative basis*
Work value	Positions	Input	Culturally sanctioned claims to status and to relative wages
Performance value	Individuals	Output (above a normal value)	Group-specific standards of effort (productivity)

Our interpretation of this framework is based on two assumptions, both of which are closely linked to the discussion in the two introductory chapters.

1   The technological and organizational development of industrial work leads to difficulties in applying the idea that a job or a particular performance of it has a specific value.[65] First, in the

[63] Euler and Stevens, 'Die analytische Arbeitsbewertung ...', 12; Fürstenberg, *Probleme der Lohnstruktur*, 82; Kosiol, *Leistungsgerechte Entlohnung*, 37.
[64] Cf. Behrend, 'The effort bargain'.
[65] Even the theoreticians of job evaluation occasionally concede that their methods are inadequate: 'In general experience shows that it is easier to develop a basic index of output in factories than in offices'; 'In the present state of scientific knowledge the area of work output which can be exactly measured is almost entirely restricted to physical demands.' Hetzler, *Die Bewertung von Bürotätigkeit*, 26, 78.

I*

different positions and the different work functions of an occupational system, the 'objective' expenditure of work is becoming more equal. Secondly, the results of work become less and less easily ascribed to individuals and less and less subject to initiatory influence, deriving instead from normatively-regulated preventive influence. Both conditions lead to the important result that the categories of work ability (qualification and performance) become increasingly unusable as a way of explaining and justifying status hierarchies.

2   However, industrial societies are characterized by their historical achievement of precisely this explanatory framework. The achievement principle makes function in the work and production sphere the decisive determinant of social status, thus becoming the fundamental model of legitimation for all social differences of income and power. In the industrial societies of the West, at least, no alternative justificatory principle is available. As a result, in these societies there is only one possible rationalization for all the status differences which have been created by cultural traditions and by economic interests—they have to be treated as if they were identical to the status differences explicable by the different qualities of individuals and the different values of work functions. The objectivistic practice of job evaluation plays an important part in this mystification. All the same, the fewer the rational starting-points job evaluation can find in the reality of industrial and bureaucratic work, the more its results become dependent upon culturally-shaped status definitions.

5   The incentive function of payment by results

So far we have been concerned with the preconditions for the operation of the achievement principle. The discussion so far has made clear that, at least if industrial work continues to develop in the way it is at the moment, it will become increasingly unlikely that these preconditions can be fulfilled. However, since the fiction that the achievement principle does operate is a central source of legitimation for the system of status distribution, it still remains nonetheless institutionally protected.

The second chapter outlined the *functions* which it is claimed the achievement principle fulfils, and which are alleged to demonstrate the principle's rationality. It is to these functions to which we must now turn. The most important of them is that of allocation, which can be subdivided into (1) the macrosociological—the allocation of labour on the labour market and (2) the microsociological—the allocation of individual output through wage differentials based on productivity. The achieving society model thus assumes that (1) the differential value of the different work functions ensures that an optimal distribution of labour is achieved by occupational choice, change and mobility: (2) the differential value which payment by results puts on individual or collective productivity stimulates those motives and interests which further an optimal fulfilment of the work task. The following analysis will be restricted to the second of these two functions,[66] i.e. to the microsociological incentive functions of wage differentials. This analysis should answer three questions: what effects do changes in industrial work have on the fulfilment of this incentive function? what functions are in fact served by institutionalized wage incentives? and finally, therefore, to what extent do the empirical consequences of applying the achievement principle support its claim to rationality?

Firstly, let us return to our critique of the belief that individual differences in performance can be determined independently of the character of the workplace. The objections to this idea are: (1) at many highly-mechanized workplaces initiatory influence has been replaced by merely preventive supervision of production, (2) in complex structures of cooperation the extent of initiatory influence is never fixed, but is limited by a multitude of continually changing conditions external to the workplace, (3) at many workplaces the quantity and the quality of output as well as material usage are all subject to the same degree of initiatory influence, so that a rise in physical productivity can always involve costs on the other two dimensions—from a business point of view it is thus of dubious value.[67]

Even if only one of these three factors has any effect on work procedures, it is enough to change the 'optimization' conditions of a production process. The organization's interests no longer demand just that output be maximized, but now also require the stabilization of those attitudes and forms of behaviour of the workers which, operating as regulatory norms, ensure that the productive equipment and the cooperative relationships of the organization function regularly, smoothly, reliably and free of conflict. The changed direction of the optimization strategy goes with the use of other methods of control—instead of using productivity bonuses to stimulate individual competitive interests, it is more effective to reduce those subjective experiences of strain, stress and loss which could hamper the creation of loyal attitudes and obedience to regulatory

[66] An exhaustive discussion of the 'macrosociological' allocation function would require an analysis of the mechanisms of occupational choice and occupational change, and in particular of the question of what role is played by them in income expectations and income differentials.
[67] These conditions explain why the effects of incentive schemes are always taken for granted, although their existence has never been decisively proved. 'It is practically impossible to obtain a definite answer to the . . . question of whether the introduction of piece rates results in increased effort and thus raises output.' H. Behrend, 'Financial incentives as a system of beliefs', *BJS* 10 (1959), 504.

norms. This strategy includes the ideological interpretation of the work relationship as one of paternalistic welfare (as expressed inter alia in the firm's social policy practice), just as much as concessions to (and thus the legitimation of) the differential income expectations which become apparent among different groups of employees as the overall organizational system maintains its economic success. Incidentally, such concessions are all the easier for the employer to make, the further wage costs have fallen as a proportion of total costs.

Theoretically, we can assume that as the level of mechanization rises, so the relationship between the use of negative and positive sanctions in the disciplining of labour changes. Relatively flexible income concessions become a more effective way of stopping the occurrence of forms of behaviour which could damage the planned functioning of production than would be the use of overt personal force and the threat to withdraw the worker's economic livelihood—the predominant methods of control in earlier industrial work situations. At the same time positive sanctions absorb all the claims to income which are *not* fixed within the framework of the status quo. Concessions in terms of income are an extremely reliable way of preventing any basic political criticism of the existing pattern of distribution, for since such concessions are based on the objectivistic pretext that income distribution is a purely 'technical' distribution mechanism, they can take into account inherited normative claims and status differences. For this reason, it is justifiable to consider the complex of positive sanctions as a form of domination, equivalent to the much more drastic and much more obvious negative sanctions of the early industrial period.

Income differentiation is therefore a technique of control which is based on work function and work performance. Such an interpretation is supported by Lutz's description of the reasons behind modern forms of wage policy in industry. According to Lutz, forms of flexible and positively-sanctioning wage policy have been introduced because

> It has been recognized that with high mechanization, an optimal productivity of labour is less likely than ever to be assured merely by pressure or by planned incentive payment systems. It follows that if the firm is to operate satisfactorily, one precondition is the existence of a certain level of loyalty or satisfaction on the part of the labour force. It further follows that even considerable wage increases have less effect on costs than for example, the careless use of raw materials, excessively long repair times or small oversights which are difficult to trace back to the individual worker. Piece work is also retained in situations where one can hardly talk of a measureable human performance. Here what is being rewarded is the smooth functioning of a group of machines— certainly productivity, but not any longer the intensity of human labour.[68]

68 Lutz, 'Hochmechanisierung und Lohnpolitik', 21.

Fürstenberg has observed how a piecerate system involving the whole of a factory fulfilled its 'incentive' function by preventing conflict behaviour rather than by creating any intensification of actual work effort. This prevention of conflict paid for itself with a considerable fall in costs, while there was no report of any increase in the quantity of goods produced. In other words, the introduction of the incentive system for the whole factory had a strong modifying influence on the peripheral rather than the central role elements of the labour force: missed shifts fell by 49·3 per cent, labour turnover by 43·5 per cent and the time needed for arbitrating disputes at work by 50 per cent.[69] However, the disciplinary success of the new incentive scheme was achieved against a background of economic crisis for the factory under study, and Fürstenberg does in fact assume that this crisis situation must have been the explanation for the success of the incentive scheme which he observed.[70]

When the possibility of initiatory influence disappears, productivity payments are based on output quantities which are the economic result of a comprehensive cooperative production process, rather than just the physical result of the intensity of the individual's work. Whenever this occurs, then the 'incentive' function of payment by results is transformed into a reward for 'disciplined' (i.e. cost-saving) behaviour.

The concrete form of incentive schemes and the way in which they operate does not depend merely on the extent to which production is mechanized. It also depends at least to the same extent on the workers' own consciousness: an effective system of productivity incentives both requires a particular form of consciousness to exist and itself develops this consciousness further. This consciousness is a complex of attitudes which can be described as *individualistic income orientation*. It exists when the workers are *willing* to modify their work behaviour (whether in terms of the intensity of their work or in terms of obedience to regulatory norms) in line with the proffered opportunities for higher incomes. At the same time, the individualistic income-orientation syndrome implies a willingness to understand the existing distribution of wages as the result of differences in performance and therefore as morally right. The syndrome assumes that there is a direct relationship between individual ability and the wage level attained, and disregards the relationships of power and exploitation which shape this relationship. To the extent that it does this, it is locked within the ruling model of legitimation provided by the achievement principle: the workers understand themselves in terms of the image of the entrepreneur who combines his factors of production in proportion to

[69] Fürstenberg, 'Die Soziale Funktion von Leistungsanreizen . . .', 112.
[70] *Ibid.*, 124.

the profit he expects, and who accepts his level of success in the market as a fair assessment of his business skill.

Whether it is meant to function by mobilizing initiative at work or by simple discipline, the operation of individually-differentiated payment by results *presupposes* that this complex of attitudes exists (the studies discussed below by Behrend, Collins, Dalton, Roy and Whyte will show how unjustified this assumption is). The mere introduction of payment by results, quite independent of any improvement in costs and in production, favours the appearance of an individualistic interpretation of wage status—those workers who accept such an interpretation of wages are now supported by an institutionalized decision in favour of an individualistic and hierarchical image of society. By itself and *prior* to any direct economic consequences, the factual institutionalization of the achievement principle then should be valuable as demonstration or indoctrination, and this too must also be considered as part of the achievement principle's disciplinary functions. By adopting such a payment system, the organization is suggesting to its employees a complex of attitudes which produce an individualistic orientation to income. However, the employees may always turn out to be immune to the suggestion. Whenever this occurs, the fulfilment of these disciplinary functions encounters an insurmountable barrier. The effectiveness of wage incentives stands or falls with the willingness of the workers to interpret these incentives actually as *incentives*. Incentive schemes

> will work as long as workers accept the proposition that standards of effort are, or ought to be, higher under financial incentive schemes and will act accordingly.[71]

This condition is no way fulfilled for all employees, but only for those with an explicitly middle-class orientation. Dalton has described in detail the sociocultural differences which are linked to the different ways in which workers react to wage incentives. He concludes:

> The social characteristics of machinists responsive to, and of those relatively indifferent to, a wage incentive scheme under which they work appear at several points to be nearly opposite to each other. Those of greatest response (1) stand at a higher educational level than others; (2) are more likely to be home owners as compared with renters among the less responsive; (3) come in most cases from families with greater economic resources and higher occupational skills and are themselves upwardly mobile (workers in the other category showing less interest in rising and having received little material or traditional impetus from their families); (4) prefer laissez faire doctrines as against empirical collectivism of the other group; and (5) behave individualistically toward

[71] Behrend, 'The effort bargain', 505.

the work group and tend to participate little in community life as measured by membership in social organization.[72]

Frequently, those workers whose sociocultural background does not predispose them to an individualistic orientation to income, perceive the time-and-motion study experts' own measuring operations as the clearest example of the conflict of power within the factory. They see the introduction of a system of payment by results based on 'normal times' for what it is, a means whereby they can be manipulated by management to ensure a maximal use of labour. As a result, this collective opposition to the attempted manipulation smothers any interest in individual wage rises. In some cases this mechanism leads to a situation in which time-and-motion studies make the conflict of power within the factory visible, producing opposition from the workers and leading to a fall in their productivity. In such cases, quite independently of the technical work conditions, the introduction of payment by results is self-contradictory : it prevents what it purports to promote without there being available (under capitalist relations of production) any alternative institutional means which could stimulate the motivation to work.

This opposition[73] of the employees is backed up by the realization that the time norms are set by the judgements of management appointees, and that these norms can at any time be changed to the worker's disadvantage. In a participant observation Roy has shown how effective such opposition is, since it is supported by informal controls within the work group.[74]

In addition to its technological inadequacy, payment by results is contradictory in two further ways.

I   Fixing time norms actualizes the conflict of power within the factory, and the workers react to this precisely by *refusing* the intensification of work which is expected of them:

> Worker responses to the incentive system depend not only upon the actual financial rewards but upon the setting of interpersonal sentiments in which these rewards are offered. Where mistrust between the parties persists, worker response to financial incentive will be half-hearted.[75]

[72] M. Dalton, 'Worker response and social background', *J. Pol. Ec.* 55 (1947), 323–32, here 331.
[73] Cf. O. Collins, M. Dalton and D. Roy, 'Restriction of output and social cleavage in industry', *Appl. Anthr.* 5 (1946), 1–14, here 8.
[74] Cf. D. Roy, 'Work satisfaction and social reward in quota achievement: an analysis of piecework incentive', *ASR* 18 (1953), 507–14; *idem*, 'Efficiency and "the fix": informal intergroup relations in a piecework machine shop', *AJS* 60 (1955), 255–66; *idem*, 'Quota restriction and gold-bricking in a machine shop', *AJS* 57 (1952); W. F. Whyte *et al.*, *Money and motivation* (New York 1955).
[75] W. F. Whyte, 'Economic incentives and human relations', *Harv. Bus. Rev.* 30 (1952), 75.

The more the basic wage itself already exceeds the culturally-defined existence minimum, however, the more the very fact of payment by results can itself have an adverse effect on 'interpersonal sentiments'. The workers will respond to the introduction of such systems by 'braking' and other forms of tacit non cooperation.

2   Technological reasons (according to Hetzler, categories for evaluating output can only be applied to physical work) and labour law traditions limit the application of incentive payments. Piece-rates and bonuses are usually only applied to those groups of employees who least satisfy the criteria of middle class consciousness which Dalton has identified as being decisive for 'positive' reaction to performance evaluation. Thus the situation occurs that individual performance is differentially assessed precisely where individualistic income orientation is least common and where the massive experience of constraint and effective intragroup controls together make incentive schemes least likely to succeed. Collins, Dalton and Roy[76] have demonstrated with qualitative material their thesis that, even in a situation where payment by results has led to a change in work behaviour, this cannot necessarily be interpreted as involving an individualistic income orientation. It cannot therefore be seen as proving the incentive function of the achievement principle. Certainly, the group of workers observed by the authors greatly preferred piecework to time wages, but not because they wanted more money:

> The machine operators did not as a group regard increased pecuniary gain as being a principal advantage of piecework.[77]

Piecework then can only increase labour productivity within narrow limits. Despite all their reservations about the practice of fixing time norms by work study, for the workers piecework is comparatively welcome. It means that monotonous and repetitive work can be structured and given a rhythm, while the worker can adopt an almost sportive distance from the work task itself:

> To these men piecework meant greater freedom to dispose of their work time as they pleased in the face of the society-wide tendency to routinize and standardize worker activities.[78]

Nonetheless, practices such as braking and the work levels that go with them remain unaltered by this relative satisfaction. Piecerate work merely provides an experience which is characterized 'by interaction, organization and completion'; it is a wage system which makes work a 'self-imposed and finished task, problem or game', while under time payment work is 'aimless, unintegrated and con-

[76] Collins, Dalton and Roy, 'Restriction of output . . .'.
[77] *Ibid.*, 7.
[78] *Ibid.*, 8.

cluded with mere cessation of activity.'[79] To the extent that the achievement principle is justified by its alleged incentive and allocative functions, the way in which these functions are transformed into a type of compensation for monotony means that the operation of incentive payment systems does not provide any arguments for the principle's validity.

In conclusion, we can now once again summarize the objections which remove the basis for any justification of the achievement principle in terms of its incentive function. Trends in the technological development of industrial work, above all the trend from initiatory to supervisory work, reduce the likelihood that the results of collective work can be differentially allocated to separate individuals. Under these conditions, the functions of the principle of payment by results is converted into an instrument of domination within the firm. However, whatever the level of development of technology, the achievement principle can still only function where the sociocultural disposition of individualistic income orientation already exists. The research results that have been cited here suggest that this condition is precisely least satisfied for those groups of workers who are most subject to payment-by-results schemes. In addition, the use of these payment systems sharpens consciousness of conflict, thus hampering their success the more the worker no longer faces immediate economic need. The great extent to which the normative pattern of individualistic income orientation is rejected is not immediately and completely obvious, but this is only because payment by results is preferred by a large part of the labour force—for reasons however which have nothing to do with the achievement principle's advertised functional legitimation.

[79] Roy, 'Work satisfaction . . .', 508.

5

Conclusion: forms and consequences of the critique of the achievement principle

The achievement principle provides a model of society in which social status is distributed equitably in line with performance. Such a model can be subjected to an empirically-based critique at three different levels.

1   According to the achieving society model, the central elements of occupational work provide the sole legitimate standard for the distribution of life-chances. The first level of critique proceeds by suggesting that the factual distribution of life-chances is actually totally at variance with this standard. The evidence for such a hypothesis is extensive. It can be taken as a basic social fact in all industrial societies that strata and classes, economic power and the irrationalities of the educational system are dominant elements of the social structure, affecting and regulating the constitution, let alone the exercise, of individual abilities. The effects of these supra-individual structural elements do not end at the boundaries of organized social institutions, but penetrate into their internal mechanisms of status distribution. To a greater or lesser extent, these effects thus reduce the possibility that existing status hier-archies can legitimate themselves as deriving from principles of status distribution which are equitable in terms of performance. If it is proven that overarching social structural determinants of status intervene within organizational hierarchies, then it is possible to see through what Dreitzel refers to as the 'self-ideologizing' of a status system and its members. However, this first type of critique of the achievement principle does not go beyond such an investigation of existing hierarchies in terms of their own specific forms of self-justification. It can show to what extent a hierarchy which bases its legitimacy on differences in performance does in fact live up to its own claims, but the legitimating norm itself lies outside the sphere of the critique: the critics themselves can even explicitly accept it or assume that it will tend increasingly to become the predominant mechanism of status distribution within industrial societies. The limitations on the questions possible within this approach preclude any statements as to the 'positive' or 'negative' (according to a

particular value system) consequences of the legitimating achievement principle itself.

2   The second level of critique tackles this question. Here it is a matter of investigating the intended and unintended results of an achievement-oriented pattern of distribution and criticizing it from within the framework of a ruling system of values and sanctioned interests. The central focus here is on the contradiction between some assumed functions of the achievement principle (individual evaluation, development of industrial productivity, a 'just' status distribution) and *other* social interests. Michael Young has described in a satire the sociological negative utopia of a society in which everyone is classified according to their intelligence quotient into a rigidly hierarchical status system.[1] In this model of society the one-dimensional nature of the fetishized norm of productivity produces a totalitarian restriction of all social processes and all forms of life which are not directly productive. In the same way Hack[2] points out the inhuman character of the achievement principle:

> A society which grades its members clearly and completely according to their contribution to increasing production makes a dubious claim to be a just society.... Linking socio-economic status to performance makes free-time almost a part of the work-sphere, so that completely irrationally work is guaranteed a clear primacy at a time when it could become (and not just quantitatively) marginal time.[3]

The development of an affluent society shaped by automated work processes makes it questionable, and not just on moral grounds, that individual living conditions and chances of consumption should be graded according to the principle of performance at work. From an economic point of view too, in an affluent society it is becoming an anachronism that the right to consumption should be tied to work performance: since automation is accompanied by open or disguised redundancies, if consumption chances are linked to the work relationship, then this must produce gaps in effective demand which would prove to be dangerous should a large amount of technical unemployment occur. This question has been raised by the authors of the manifesto of the 'Triple Revolution':

> The industrial system does not possess any adequate mechanisms to permit the potentials (of cybernation) to become realities.... The continuance of the income-through-jobs link as the only major mechanism for distributing effective demand—for granting the right to consume—now acts as the main break on the almost unlimited capacity of a cybernated production system.[4]

[1](M. Young, *The rise of the meritocracy* (London 1958).
[2] L. Hack, 'Was heisst schon Leistungsgesellschaft?', *Neue Kritik* 7(35) (1966), 23–32.
[3] *Ibid.*, 28–9.
[4] *The triple revolution*, 7.

If not only the *level* of labour income depends on characteristics of occupational position, but even the very possibility of having an income is identical with the technologically-determined possibility of realizing one's own labour power, then industrial progress will be restricted, at least in those sections where it is dependent on consumers' demand which declines with unemployment (and to a lesser extent certainly also with 'downgrading' in the qualification structure). Thus in a paradoxical fashion, and in opposition to its original sociopolitical intention, the institutionalized achievement principle hampers rather than furthers the development of the productive forces of industrial societies.

The practical consequences of the economic argument suggest that as economic citizens everyone must be granted a right to consumption which is guaranteed by state income-redistribution policies. If technological unemployment is not to lead to a fall in demand with Depression-type consequences, or if unemployment is not to be absorbed by unproductive investment in armaments and prestige science, then this right to consumption will have to go far beyond the right to a minimum level of civilized existence.

Bahrdt is also concerned with the irrationality of the normative model of the achieving society when he describes its violation by mechanisms which make promotion dependent on length of service (the seniority principle).[5] For Bahrdt such a system reduces stress and is therefore beneficial. To a certain extent this form of what he calls the 'socialization of promotion chances' could in fact reduce the neurotic threat to identity which results from the imperative of mobility through achievement.[6] Nonetheless, it clearly remains debatable whether the seniority principle and its beneficial effects are in fact a relic of pre-industrial patterns of status distribution, so that its survival is merely a delay in adaptation, or whether the achievement principle has actually been seen to be repressive, so that the seniority principle really does represent a conscious counter-institution to it.

Finally, in his analysis of the normative and technically unjustifiable basis of the wage differentials between positions, Baldamus[7] expects that the justification of wages by performance will gradually dissolve: 'it is becoming increasingly likely that the principle of recompense for effort will finally itself be challenged', once it is recognized that the wage structure is determined by position-specific claims and 'standards of suitability', and once it is seen as fictitious to justify these by differential amounts of work effort.

Sooner or later the workers will make the discovery that there is no

[5] Bahrdt, *Industrieburokratie*, 123.
[6] Cf. Luckmann and Berger, 'Social mobility and personal identity'.
[7] Baldamus, *Der gerechte Lohn*.

logical necessity in the relationship of effort and wages. They will see that in reality it is only an historically accidental cultural relationship. The question of what wage is suitable for what amount of daily work weariness unavoidably leads to the more radical question—has this remarkable calculation any sense at all, if at the end of the day the suitability is only a question of whatever accidental customary convention happens to be operating?[8]

All the objections to the achievement principle that have just been outlined are not concerned with the fact that the principle is not completely realized in reality. Rather, they all focus on precisely the consequences of its all-too-complete success—in as much as, that is, these consequences conflict with existing interests and values. This form of critique has a moral basis—it points out the 'costs' that a society must be prepared to pay if it accepts the achievement principle as a 'just' mechanism by which to distribute status. Given the inhuman consequences of a full realization of the achievement principle, the critique then challenges the principle's own claim to validity. Of course, a sociological critique of the achievement principle remains abstract and moralistic if it does not also investigate the *suitability* of the achievement norm to the concrete form of work organizations and if it does not make *this* subject to empirical discussion.

3   The question this study has posed and answered in the negative is whether the idea of an all-pervasive scale of performance is in any way suitable to the technologically and organizationally determined exercise of industrial and bureaucratic occupational work. First, the extent of initiatory influence on the work result is declining; secondly, the proportion of regulatory norms in the work role is increasing; thirdly, the discontinuous distribution of tasks within work organizations reduces the 'demonstration chance' of the individual skill; fourthly, the general expansion of formal educational processes, together with the fact that technology is making 'nature-near' tasks less onerous, leads to a levelling out of position-specific work effort; fifthly, in complex work organizations it is as impossible to determine each individual's productivity as it is to locate a position's functional importance. If these facts mark a *developmental trend* in industrial and bureaucratic work, then the validity of the achievement principle is becoming factually debatable and its claim to validity is revealed as politically and morally untenable. It also follows that objective and social structural reasons lead to the operational disintegration of the concept of performance. Even as a prescriptive norm, therefore, the achievement principle itself becomes meaningless.

The achievement principle remains nevertheless institutionally

[8] *Ibid.*, 77.

sanctioned; but to the extent to which it has lost its social structural correlates, its point of departure shifts from the category of achievement to a series of substitute criteria, predominantly the normative dimensions of the individuals work behaviour. As a result the achievement principle is changing its function. Under early industrial conditions it was a procedure which specified the differential labour power of individuals, and as such could claim some rationality—at least as far as increasing productivity was concerned. Now, however, it is turning into a disciplinary technique which rewards loyalty to the dominant interests and forms of life. It perpetuates cultural divisions and creates and stabilizes the appearance of an objective or 'technical' legitimacy of organizational hierarchies. Originally, then, the principle aimed at a society which was equitable in terms of achievement, and as the function of the principle changes, so its original intention is violated.

However, this is not the only reason why the normative model of the achievement principle is becoming meaningless. Given its change of function, it cannot today be argued that the achievement principle guarantees the optimal use of all productive resources and the equitable distribution of goods and services among individuals with equal rights. The second type of critique makes clear the impossibility of any such claim. However, the concept of a social order which is equitable in terms of performance really first becomes *meaningless* when we consider the fact that advanced forms of industrial work make the category of individual skill as revealed in competition simply irrelevant. As we have seen, it is for this reason that both organizational promotion procedures and individuals' corresponding subjective strategies have to have recourse to substitute criteria. These not only lack the 'objective meaning' of the achievement principle, but also abandon the formal definition of achievement as the individual, gradable and comparable performance of work.[9]

From rather different premises, Tumin, in an afterword to the debate over the functionalist theory of stratification, has queried the validity of a mechanism based on allocating differential social rewards to differential work functions.[10] Tumin's argument can be used to discuss the thesis that the achievement principle has undergone a change of function and that therefore the concept of performance has become obsolete.

Tumin contrasts work and parenthood roles, distinguishing as separate elements of the work role regulatory norms (summarized as 'conscientiousness') and the technical aptitude corresponding to the particular work function ('talent' in the language of function-

---

[9] Compare the distinction between technical and normative rules made in the first chapter of this study.

[10] M. M. Tumin, 'Rewards and task orientation'.

alist stratification theory). The fulfilment of the parent role is socially controlled, in that in the rearing of children positive sanctions are awarded to care and conscientiousness. By contrast, in the work role the extent of the specific ability and knowledge becomes the means of social control: 'more' talented individuals receive more power, privilege and income than 'less' talented ones. The functionalist theory of stratification claims that the differential evaluation of individual abilities is by itself an adequate control mechanism to ensure that the most effective possible distribution of labour occurs within a system of division of labour. If this were the case, then ranking a position higher would also ensure a higher level of conscientiousness in its fulfilment:

> If one assumes—as does the traditional view of stratification—that men of different talents cannot be adequately motivated except by differential rewards ... then there should be far more conscientiousness shown by the average employee at his job than by the average parent in his family tasks.[11]

The opposite is obviously the case: a fact which shows that the motivational power of differential rewards assumed by functionalist theory is in fact inadequate to explain how work roles are fulfilled. From this it follows that the functionalist position cannot explain social stratification itself, since differentiating status according to performance ability does not solve the problem of allocation. What then are the control mechanisms which do ensure that work tasks are fulfilled? How are those conditions created

> which impel men to be conscientious at their tasks, i.e. willing to do the most of which they are capable rather than the least with which they can get by?[12]

Tumin proposes a solution which would put the system of status distribution on a new basis:

> Nothing would make it less efficient to reward according to conscientiousness rather than acccording to differential talent. ... If it is conscientiousness which one seeks to maximize, then clearly it is this principle rather than biologically inherited talent which ought to be the central criterion in the reward system.[13]

This formal construction of an alternative distribution mechanism seems especially sensible from the point of view of the argument of this study, namely that there has been a relative increase in those role elements which we have defined as regulatory norms. Since structural change in the typical work situation has made the concept of performance inadequate, Tumin's argument can be interpreted as an attempt to revitalize the concept by deliberately

[11] *Ibid.*, 421.
[12] *Ibid.*, 419.
[13] *Ibid.*, 421.

changing its focus. Tumin is proposing that the allocation of differential status to individuals should depend on normative categories
rather than on the central and technical ones. This proposal
amounts to replacing the traditional achievement principle with a
modified version. Nonetheless, the new version is inconsistent and
impractical for the following reasons:

1   Taking the parent role as a point of comparison has made
Tumin lose sight of the fact that cooperative work systems require
more than just general 'functional talents' such as 'conscientiousness'. At least in addition to these, specific forms of behaviour with
materials and with role partners become very important, and these
are learnt in training and at the workplace itself. The 'professional
culture' of doctors and lawyers, the 'technical sensibility' of workers
in mechanized production and the 'contact ability' of clerical
workers are all examples which demonstrate that the different
regulatory norms required for specialized work tasks cannot be
simply reduced to the common denominator of 'conscientiousness'
in order to reconstruct the organizational status structure.

2   As we have seen, one characteristic of the 'internal' controls
which enter into work behaviour is that they cannot be 'more' or
'less' present: whether they are followed or not has to be judged
according to a yes/no criterion.[14] Unlike the case of the parent role,
the specific requirements of the work role only permit a very limited
variation in the form and extent of the normatively guided work
performance. The individual is certainly required to follow autonomously a normative pattern, but the organization is so vulnerable
to deviations that no noticeable shortfalls in the extent to which the
norms are fulfilled can be allowed, while any overfulfilment of the
norm is equally rather meaningless. As a result, conscientiousness
is useless as a measure by which to judge relative status in a work
organization.

3   As Baldamus above all has stressed, regulatory norms which
are part of behaviour at the workplace comprise a contribution to
the employer by society as a whole, one which has been created in
the socialization process. For this reason, labour power cannot be
understood as an abstract general human quality, but has to be
seen as arising from different subcultural socialization and educational conditions. How the members of an organization behave
vis-à-vis their role partners and with the objects of their work all
depends to a very small extent on the material rewards which the
organization offers them for their behaviour; the readiness to react
to differential rewards with a change of work behaviour is far more
the result of the specific conditions under which the individual has
been socialized. Tumin's proposed status distribution mechanism

[14] Cf. p. 121 above.

is therefore as unable to solve the problem of allocation as the mechanism assumed to exist by functionalist stratification theory. In general, obedience to regulatory norms cannot be understood as a reaction to proffered rewards, but only as the relatively rigid result of previous educational and socialization processes.

4   Tumin's reward mechanism is meant to ensure a high level of identification with the work task, but the chief reason why it cannot do this is that the very existence of differential rewards can *prevent* the functional regulation of work behaviour from operating. If income from work and occupational status are both differentiated according to the characteristics of the work role, this makes members of the work organization interpret their own work behaviour as an integral part of a process of exchange which has no normative obligations. This exchange relationship will lead the employees to develop organizational identities and loyalties in exchange for rewards and in order to improve their social status, but this can only happen so long as the employees have an individualistic attitude to income and mobility. By contrast, with those groups which are not characterized by an individualistic status consciousness, the very retention of the exchange model of status distribution could prevent them from accepting regulatory norms as binding. We have already seen from studies of the ways in which incentives operate that large groups of employees are not interested enough in improving their individual status to ensure that these normative forces are utilized. The same applies to the growing number of 'professional' occupations in which status motives, rather than stimulating obedience to the 'regulative code of ethics', actually hinder it. With his proposal Tumin is attempting to restore a situation which now no longer exists in wide areas of work in industrial society, namely one in which desires for occupational status and the rules of occupational action were in a liberal harmony with each other, such that status interests were the most effective way of ensuring the required work behaviour.

The professions are only the clearest example of an opposition between the principle of exchange and a functional exercise of the occupation. While the exchange principle attempts to control work behaviour by the traditional mechanisms of payment and relative discrimination, if it is retained it blocks the development of that self-evaluative regulation of work performance which plays such an important role in ever larger areas of industrial and bureaucratic work.

Tumin's modified model of the achieving society clearly fails to grasp how inadequate the concept of performance is in the structural conditions of industrial organizations. There are clearly other possible alternatives to Tumin's proposal apart from a model which postulates that status attributes should be mechanically equally distributed through the work organizations. Another possibility, also the result of drawing the consequences from this critique of the achievement principle, would be a system of status distribution in which social status was *separated* from the characteristics of the work role and *sanctioned* at the political level. We have already seen that today the differences between the labour incomes of the different occupational positions can only be explained by the parallel existence of, first, an accepted hierarchy of values and secondly, the traditional differences in the level of claims made by the different occupational groups. Nonetheless, this normative basis of the income structure is overlaid with technical fictions and rationalizations. These serve the function of describing the status differences between working individuals as the result of relative failures of merit, thus distracting from the normative, but unexplicated, value hierarchy which actually ranks the different work functions. The institutionally-fixed yet nonetheless fictitious criteria of the differential value of work functions become all the more absurd the less—in discontinuous organizations—the 'higher' positions can be described as 'multiples' of the requirements made of the subordinate members of the organization.

This contradiction between the fiction of a technical determination of income and the fact of its normative distribution could be resolved in a model of distribution which put the normative value hierarchy under the control of the political level, thus making the distribution of income and of social opportunities a process of public decision. Certainly in such a process the criteria of distribution would then no longer be the costs or productivity of individual labour, but rather the politically-sanctioned needs of both the working and the nonworking groups of the population.

In such a system, status would be allocated on the basis of politically-determined needs, and this could make redundant both the pretence that status is technically determined and the desire for individual status. Neither of these is now supported any longer by any argument of economic rationality—they do not fulfil their 'incentive function', they force conformity with extrafunctional orientations, while personnel recruitment through occupational mobility is becoming increasingly irrational. If the achieving society model of status distribution were also to be replaced in the *self-consciousness* of industrial societies by politically-determined status guarantees, this change would be completely in line with a reversal of the direction of development of industrial societies that has occasionally been diagnosed : namely that the trend from 'status to contract' is being replaced by one 'from contract to status'.[15] How-

[15] Cf. T. H. Marshall, *Class, citizenship and social development* (New York 1963); P. F. Drucker, 'The employee society', *AJS* 58 (1952), 358–63.

ever, since this reversal, while removing the disciplinary functions of the achievement principle, at the same time could still motivate the necessary functional obedience to regulatory norms, it need in no way have any regressive aspects.

Abbreviations

Adm. Sc. Quart.	Administrative Science Quarterly
AJS	American Journal of Sociology
Am. Ec. Rev.	American Economic Review
Am. J. Econ. and Soc.	American Journal of Economics and Sociology
Appl. Anthr.	Applied Anthropology
Arch. f. Soz. wiss. u. Soz. pol.	Achiv für Soziallwissenschaft und Sozialpolitik
ASR	American Sociological Review
BJS	British Journal of Sociology
Eur. Arch. f. Soz.	Europäisches Archiv für Sociologie
FH	Frankfurter Hefte
GMh	Gewerkschaftliche Monatshefte
Harv. Bus. Rev.	Harvard Business Review
Hmb. Jb.	Hamburger Jahrbuch für Wirtschafts- und Gesellschaftspolitik
Hum. Rel.	Human Relations
Ind. and Lab. Rel. Rev.	Industrial and Labor Relations Review
Int. Lab. Rev.	International Labour Review
Int. Soc. J.	International Socialist Journal
J. Am. Med. Assoc.	Journal of the American Medical Association
J. Pol. Ec.	Journal of Political Economy
Jb. f. Nat. ök. u. Stat.	Jahrbücher für Nationalökonomie und Statistik
Jb. f. Soz. wiss.	Jahrbuch für Socialwissenschaft
KZfSS	Kölner Zeitschrift für Soziologie und Sozialpsychologie
Psych. Bull.	Psychological Bulletin
Schw. . f. Volksw. u. Stat.	Schweizerische Zeitschrift für Volkswirtschaft und Statistik
Soc. Forc.	Social Forces
Soc. Res.	Social Research

References

ACHINGER, H. 1958: *Sozialpolitik als Gesellschaftspolitik.* Hamburg.

BAHRDT, H. P. 1956: 'Fiktiver Zentralismus in Grossunternehmungen', *Kyklos* **9**, 483ff.

1958: *Industriebürokratie.* Stuttgart.

1960a: 'Arbeitssoziologische Aspekte des technischen Fortschritts in der Industrieverwaltung', *Hmb. Jb.* **5**, 58–68.

1960b: 'Die Krise der Hierarchie im Wandel der Kooperationsformen', *Proceedings of the 14th Congress of German Sociologists.* Stuttgart.

BAKKE, E. W. 1940: *Citizens without work.* New Haven, Conn.

BALDAMUS, W. 1951: 'Type of work and motivation', *BJS* **2**, 44–58.

1960: *Der gerechte Lohn.* Berlin.

1961: *Efficiency and effort.* London.

BARAN, P. A. and SWEEZY, P. M. 1967: *Monopoly capital.* New York.

BARBER, B. 1957: *Social stratification.* New York.

BATES, F. L. and PELLEGRIN, H. J. 1959–60: 'Congruity and incongruity of status attributes within occupations and work positions', *Soc. Forc.* **38**, 23–8.

BEALE, L. V. and KRIESBERG, L. 1959: 'Career-relevant values of medical students', *J. Am. Med. Assoc.* **171**, 1447ff.

BECKER, H. S. 1956: 'The development of identification with an occupation', *AJS* **61**, 289–98.

BECKER, H. S. and CARPER, J. 1956: 'The elements of identification with an occupation', *ASR* **21**, 341–8.

BECKER, H. S. and STRAUSS, A. L. 1956: 'Careers, personality and adult socialization', *AJS* **62**, 253–63.

BEHREND, H. 1957: 'The effort bargain', *Ind. and Lab. Rel. Rev.* **10**.

1959: 'Financial incentives as a system of beliefs', *BJS* **10**.

BENDIX, R. 1960: *Herrschaft und Industriearbeit.* Frankfurt a.M.

BENSMAN, J. and GERVER, J. 1953–4: 'Towards a sociology of expertness', *Soc. Forc.* **32**, 226–35.

BENSMAN, J. and ROSENBERG, B. 1960: 'The meaning of work in bureaucratic society', in M. Stein, A. Vidich and D. White (eds.), *Identity and Anxiety.* New York, 181–97.

BENSMAN, J. and VIDICH, A. 1962: 'Power cliques in bureaucratic society', *Soc. Res.* **29**, 467–74.

BLAU, P. M. 1964: *Exchange and power in social life.* New York.

BRAYFIELD, A. H. and CROCKETT, W. H. 1955: 'Employee attitudes and employee performance' *Psych. Bull.* **52**, 396–428.

BROOM, L. and SMITH, J. H. 1963: 'Bridging occupations', *BJS* **14**, 321–34.
BUCKLOW, M. 1966: 'A new role for the work group', *Adm. Sc. Quart.* **11**, 59–78.

CAPLOW, T. 1954: *The sociology of work*. Minneapolis.
CHINOY, E. 1952: 'The tradition of opportunity and the aspirations of automobile workers', *AJS* **57**, 453–9.
   1955: 'Social mobility trends in the United States', *ASR* **20**, 180–86.
CLAESSENS, D., FUHRMANN, J., HARTFIELD, G. and ZIRWAS, H. 1960: *Arbeiter und Angestellte in der Betriebspyramide*, ed. O. Stammer. Berlin.
COATES, C. H. and PELLEGRIN, R. J. 1956: 'Executives and supervisors: a situational theory of differential occupational mobility', *Soc. Forc.* **35**, 121–6.
   1957–8: 'Executives and supervisors: informal factors in differential bureaucratic promotion', *Adm. Sc. Quart.* **2**, 200–215.
   1962: 'Executives and supervisors: contrasting self-conceptions and conceptions of each other', in B. H. Stoodley (ed.), *Society and self*. New York, 48ff.
COLLINS, O. 1946: 'Ethnic behavior in industry', *AJS* **51**, 293–8.
COLLINS, O., DALTON, M. and ROY, D. 1946: 'Restriction of output and social cleavage in industry', *Appl. Anthr.* **5**, 1–14.
CROCKETT, H. 1962: 'The achievement motive and differential mobility in the United States', *ASR* **27**, 191–204.

DAHRENDORF, R. 1956: 'Industrielle Fertigkeiten und soziale Schichtung', *KZfSS* **8**, 540–68.
   1965: *Industrie- und Betriebssoziologie*. Berlin.
DALTON, M. 1947: 'Worker response and social background', *J. Pol. Ec.* **55**, 323–32.
   1950: 'Informal factors in career achievement', *AJS* **56**, 407–15.
   1959: *Men who manage*. New York.
   1964: 'Conflict between staff and line managerial officers', in A. Etzioni (ed.), *Complex organizations*. New York, 212ff.
DAVIES, A. F. 1952: 'Prestige of occupations', *BJS* **3**, 134–47.
DAVIS, K. 1966: 'Reply to Tumin', in R. Bendix and S. M. Lipset (eds.), *Class, status and power*. 2nd edn, New York, 59–62.
DAVIS, K. and MOORE, W. E. 1966: 'Some principles of stratification', in R. Bendix and S. M. Lipset (eds.), *Class, status and power*. 2nd edn, New York, 47–53.
DICHGANS, H. 1963: *Die Dauer der Ausbildung für akademische Berufe: Schriftenreihe des Stifterverbandes zur Förderung der Wissenschaft*. Essen.
DREITZEL, H. P. 1962: *Elitebegriff und Sozialstruktur*. Stuttgart.
DREYFUSS, C. 1962: 'Prestige grading: a mechanism of control', in R. K. Merton (ed.), *Reader in bureaucracy*. New York, 258–64.
DRUCKER, P. F. 1952: 'The employee society', *AJS* **58**, 358–63.

EATON, J. 1951: 'Social processes of professional teamwork', *ASR* **16**, 363–74.
ETZIONI, A. 1964: 'Industrial sociology: the study of economic organizations', in Etzioni (ed.), *Complex organizations*. New York, 130–42.
EULER, H. and STEVENS, H. 1952: *Die analytische Arbeitsbewertung als Hilfsmittel zur Bestimmung der Arbeitsschwierigkeit*. Düsseldorf.

FAUNCE, W. A. 1958: 'Automation in the automobile industry: some consequences for in-plant social structure', *ASR* **23**, 401–7.

FAUNCE, W. A. and SHEPPARD, H. L. 1956: 'Automation: some consequences for industrial relations', *Transactions of the 3rd World Congress of Sociology*. London, II, 165ff.

FOA, U. G. 1954: 'Types of formal leaders: their role-perception and in-group contacts', *Transactions of the 2nd World Congress of Sociology*. London, I, 110–14.

FOOTE, N. N. 1952: 'The professionalization of labor in Detroit', *AJS* **58**, 371–80.

1956: 'The movement from jobs to careers in American industry', *Transactions of the 3rd World Congress of Sociology*. London, II, 30–40.

FORM, W. H. and MILLER, D. C. 1959: 'Occupational career patterns as a sociological instrument', *AJS* **54**, 317–29.

FRIEDMANN, E. A. and HAVINGHURST, R. J. 1954: *The meaning of work and retirement*. Chicago.

FRIEDRICHS, G. (ed.) 1965: *Automation—Risiko und Chance*. 2 vols, Frankfurt a.M.

FROOMKIN, J. and JAFFE, A. J. 1953: 'Occupational skill and socio-economic structure', *AJS* **59**, 42–8.

FÜRSTENBERG, F. 1958: *Probleme der Lohnstruktur*. Tübingen.

1959: 'Die soziale Funktion von Leistungsanreizen im Industriebetrieb', in P. Atteslander (ed.), *Konflikt und Kooperation im Industriebetrieb*. Cologne/Opladen.

1962: *Das Aufstiegsproblem in der modernen Gesellschaft*. Stuttgart.

GALBRAITH, J. K. 1967: *The new industrial state*. New York.

GANGULI, C. H. 1961: *Industrial productivity and motivation*. Bombay.

GEHLEN, A. 1952: 'Probleme einer soziologischen Handlungslehre', in C. Brinkmann (ed.), *Soziologie und Leben*. Tübingen, 28–59.

1956: *Urmensch und Spätkultur*. Bonn.

GEMBARDT, U. 1959: 'Akademische Ausbildung und Beruf', *KZfSS* **11**, 223–45.

GERVER, I. and BENSMAN, J. 1954: 'Toward a sociology of expertness', *Soc. Forc.* **32**, 226–35.

GLICK, P. C. and MILLER, H. P. 1956: 'Educational level and potential income', *ASR* **21**, 307–12.

GOODMAN, P. S. 1967: 'An empirical examination of Elliott Jaques' concept of time span', *Hum. Rel.* **20**, 155–80.

GOULDNER, A. W. 1954: *Patterns of industrial bureaucracy*. Glencoe, Ill.

1965: 'Organizational analysis', in R. K. Merton, L. Broom and L. Cottrell (eds.), *Sociology today*. New York, II, 400–428.

GREENWOOD, E. 1962: 'Attributes of a profession', in S. Nosow and W. H. Form (eds.), *Men, work and society*. New York, 206–18.

GUEST, R. H. 1954: 'Work careers and aspirations of automobile workers', *ASR* **19**, 155–63.

HABERMAS, J. 1968: *Wissenschaft und Technik als 'Ideologie'?* Frankfurt a.M. Title essay of this collection translated as 'Science and technology as "ideology",' in J. Habermas, *Knowledge and human interests*, London, 1972.

HACK, L. 1966: 'Was heisst schon Leistungsgesellschaft', *Neue Kritik* **7**(35), 23–32.

HARTMANN, H. 1959: *Authority and organization in German management.* Princeton.

1964: 'Bürokratische und voluntaristische Dimensionen im organisierten Sozialgebilde', *Jb. f. Soz. wiss.* **15**, 115ff.

1965: *Funktionale Autorität.* Stuttgart.

HEILBRONNER, R. 1967: *The limits of American capitalism.* New York.

HEITBAUM, H. 1955: 'Vom Arbeitswert zum Lohn', *GMh* **6**.

1956: 'Lohnermittlung bei fortschreitender Rationalisierung und Automation', *WWI-Mitteilungen* **9**.

HERTZLER, J. O. 1952: 'Some tendencies towards a closed class system in the United States', *Soc. Forc.* **30**, 313–23.

HETZLER, H. W. 1961: *Die Bewertung von Bürotätigkeiten: Grundlagen und Verfahren.* Cologne/Opladen.

HOFFMANN, R. 1966: 'Produktivität als Fetisch: gewerkschaftliche Motive einer indexgebundenen Lohnpolitik', *FH* **21**, 765–73.

HOFMANN, W. 1965: *Einkommenstheorie.* Berlin.

HUGHES, E. C. 1965: 'The study of occupations', in R. K. Merton, L. Broom and L. Cottrell (eds.), *Sociology today.* New York, 442–60.

HYMAN, H. 1953: 'The value system of different classes', in R. Bendix and S. M. Lipset (eds.), *Class, status and power.* New York, 420–42.

ICHHEISER, G. 1930: *Kritik des Erfolges.* Leipzig.

IFO-INSTITUT FÜR WIRTSCHAFTSFORSCHUNG 1962: *Soziale Auswirkungen des technischen Fortschritts.* Berlin/Munich.

INSTITUT FÜR SOZIALFORSCHUNG 1955: *Betriebsklima.* Frankfurt a.M.

JAQUES, E. 1956: *Measurement of responsibility: a study of work payment and individual capacity.* London.

KATZ, D. 1954: 'Satisfactions and deprivations in industrial life', in A. Kornhauser, R. Dubin and A. Ross (eds.), *Industrial conflict.* New York, 86–106.

KEAT, P. G. 1960: 'Long run change in occupational wage structure, 1900–1956', *Am. J. Pol. Ec.* **68**, 584–600.

KLUTH, H. 1965: 'Amtsgedanke und Pflichtethos in der Industriegesellschaft', *Hmb. Jb.* **10**, 11–22.

KRELLE, W. 1950: 'Die Grenzproduktivitätstheorie des Lohnes', *Jb. f. Nat. ök. u. Stat.* 162.

KRIESBERG, L. 1962: 'The bases of occupational prestige: the case of dentists', *ASR* **27**, 238–44.

KOSIOL, E. 1962: *Leistungsgerechte Entlohnung.* Wiesbaden.

KUBAT, D. 1963: 'Social mobility in Czechoslovakia', *ASR* **28**, 203–12.

LENSKI, G. 1966: *Power and privilege.* New York.

LESTER, R. A. 1951: 'A range theory of wage-differentials', *Ind. and Lab. Rel. Rev.* **5**.

LIPSET, S. M. and BENDIX, R. 1952: 'Social mobility and occupational career patterns', *AJS* **57**, 366–74, 494–504.

1959: *Social mobility in industrial society.* Berkeley.

LIPSET, S. M. and MALM, F. T. 1955: 'First jobs and career patterns', *Am. J. Econ. and Soc.* **14**, 247–61.

LIVERNASH, E. R. 1953: 'Stabilization of internal wage rate structure', *Ind. and Lab. Rel. Rev.* **7**.

1954: 'Wage administration and production standards', in A. Kornhauser, R. Dubin and A. Ross (eds.), *Industrial conflict*. New York, 330–44.

LOCKWOOD, D. 1958: *The blackcoated worker*. London.

LOVENSTEIN, M. 1966: 'Guaranteed income and traditional economics', in R. Theobald (ed.), *The guaranteed income*. New York.

LUCKMANN, T. and BERGER, P. 1964: 'Social mobility and personal identity', *Eur. Arch. f. Soz.* **5**, 331–44.

LUTZ, B. 1961 and 1962: 'Hochmechanisierung und Lohnpolitik', *Atomzeitalter* 1961(12) and 1962(1).

LUTZ, B. and WILLENER, A. 1959: *Mechanisierungsgrad und Entlohnungsform: zusammenfassender Bericht*. Luxemburg.

MARSH, R. M. 1961: 'Formal organization and promotion in a pre-industrial society', *ASR* **26**, 547–56.

MARSHALL, T. H. 1963: *Class, citizenship, and social development*. New York.

MARX, K. 1875: 'Kritik des Gothaer Programms', reprinted in vol. 3 of K. Marx and F. Engels, *Selected works*. 3 vols, Moscow 1970, 9–30.

MAYNTZ, R. 1958: 'Begriff und empirische Fassung des sozialen Status in der heutigen Soziologie', *KZfSS* **10**, 58–73.

1961: 'Kritische Bemerkungen zur funktionalistischen Schichtungstheorie', *KZfSS* **5**, 10–28.

MAYO, E. 1952: *The social problems of an industrial civilization*. London.

MECHANIC, D. 1962: 'Sources of power of lower participants in complex organizations', *Adm. Sc. Quart.* **7**, 349–64.

MERTON, R. K. 1940: 'Bureaucratic structure and personality', *Soc. Forc.* **17**, 560–68.

1962: 'The machine, the worker and the engineer', in S. Nosow and W. H. Form (eds.), *Man, work and society*. New York, 82–7.

MILLER, D. C. and FORM, W. H. 1955: *Industrial sociology: the sociology of work organizations*. New York.

MILLS, C. W. 1956: *White collar*. New York.

1958: *The power elite*. New York.

MORSE, N. C. and WEISS, R. S. 1955: 'The function and meaning of work and the job', *ASR* **20**, 191–8.

MUNTZ, E. E. 1955: 'The decline of wage differentials based on skill in the United States', *Int. Lab. Rev.* **71**.

NEGT, O. 1967: 'In Erwartung der autoritären Leistungsgesellschaft', in G. Schäfer and C. Nedelmann (eds.), *Der CDU-Staat*. Munich, 200–237.

NOSOW, S. 1962: 'Labor distribution and the normative system', in S. Nosow and W. H. Form (eds.), *Man, work and society*. New York, 117–26.

OFFE, C. 1969: 'Politische Herrschaft und Klassenstrukturen', in G. Kress and D. Senghaas (eds.), *Politikwissenschaft*. Frankfurt a.M., 155–89.

PARSONS, T. 1951: *The social system*. New York.

POLLOCK, F. 1964: *Automation.* Frankfurt a.M.

POPITZ, H., BAHRDT, H. P., JÜRES, A. and KESTING, H. 1957a: *Das Gesellschaftsbild des Arbeiters.* Tübingen.

1957b: *Technik und Industriearbeit.* Stuttgart.

PREISER, E. 1955: 'Erkenntniswert und Grenzen der Grenzproduktivitätstheorie', *Schw. Z̧. f. Volksw. u. Stat.* **89.**

REDER, W. 1955: 'The theory of occupational wage differentials', *Am. Ec. Rev.* **45.**

REICHWEIN, R. 1965: *Funktionswandlungen der betrieblichen Sozialpolotik.* Cologne/Opladen.

REYNOLDS, L. 1951: *The structure of labor markets.* New York.

RIDGEWAY, V. F. 1967: 'Dysfunctional consequences of performance measurements', in W. A. Hill and D. M. Evans (eds.), *Readings in organization theory.* Boston.

RIESMAN, D. 1960: *Die einsame Masse.* Hamburg. English original is *The lonely crowd,* New Haven, 1965.

ROGOFF, N. 1957: 'Recent trends in occupational mobility', in P. K. Hatt and A. J. Reiss (eds.), *Cities and society.* 2nd edn, New York, 432–45.

ROPER, E. 1951–2: 'Discrimination in industry: extravagant injustice', *Ind. and Lab. Rel. Rev.* **5,** 584–9.

ROSEN, B. C. 1956: 'The achievement syndrone: a psychocultural dimension of social stratification', *ASR* **21,** 203–11.

ROSENBERG, M. 1957: *Occupations and values.* New York.

ROWNTREE, J. and ROWNTREE, M. 1968: 'Youth as a class', *Int. Soc. J.* **5,** 25–59.

ROY, D. 1952: 'Quota restriction and goldbricking in a machine shop', *AJS* **57.**

1953: 'Work satisfaction and social reward in quota achievement: an analysis of piecework incentive', *ASR* **18,** 507–14.

1955: 'Efficiency and "the fix": informal intergroup relations in a piecework machine shop', *AJS* **60,** 255–66.

SCHAEFER, W. 1954: 'Lohnpolitik und Lohntechnik', *GMh* **5.**

SCHEIN, E. H. and OTT, J. S. 1961: 'The legitimacy of organizational influence', *AJS* **67,** 682–9.

SCHNEIDER, L. and DORNBUSCH, S. M. 1953: 'The deferred gratification pattern: a preliminary study', *ASR* **18,** 142–8.

SCHUMPETER, J. A. 1916–17: 'Das Grundprinzip der Verteilungstheorie', *Arch. f. Soz. wiss. u. Soz. pol.* **42.**

SEEMAN, M. and EVANS, J. W. 1961: 'Apprenticeship and attitude change', *AJS* **67,** 365–78.

SHIMMIN, S. 1959: *Payment by results.* London.

SIEBEL, W. 1964: 'Berufsqualifikation im automatisierten Industriebetrieb', *Soziale Welt* **15,** 4.

SIMMONS, O. G. 1965: *Work and mental illness.* New York.

SIMON, H. A. 1945: *Administrative behavior.* New York.

1952: 'Decision making and administrative organization', in R. K. Merton (ed.), *Reader in bureaucracy.* New York, 185–94.

SIMPSON, R. L. and SIMPSON, I. H. 1960: 'Correlates and estimation of occupational prestige', *AJS* **66,** 135–40.

SLOCUM, W. L. 1966: *Occupational careers.* Chicago.

SMIGEL, E. O. 1960: 'The impact of recruitment on the organization of the large law firm', *ASR* **25**, 56–66.

STINCHCOMBE, A. L. 1966: 'Some empirical consequences of the Davis-Moore theory of stratification', in R. Bendix and S. M. Lipset (eds.), *Class, status and power.* 2nd edn, New York, 69–73.

STONE, R. C. 1953: 'Mobility factors as they affect workers' attitudes and conduct toward incentive systems', *ASR* **17**, 58–64.

1953: 'Factory organization and vertical mobility', *ASR* **18**, 28–35.

The triple revolution: manifesto of the ad hoc committee on the triple revolution. Santa Barbara, 1964.

THEOBALD, R. (ed.) 1966: *The guaranteed income.* New York.

TUMIN, M. M. 1955: 'Rewards and task orientation', *ASR* **20**.

1966: 'Some principles of stratification: a critical analysis', in R. Bendix and S. M. Lipset (eds.), *Class, status and power.* 2nd edn, New York.

VOLLMER, H. M. and MILLS, D. L. (eds.) 1966: *Professionalization.* Englewood Cliffs, NJ.

VROOM, V. H. 1964: *Work and motivation.* New York.

WALKER, C. E. 1952: *The man in the assembly line.* Cambridge, Mass.

1958: *Toward the automatic factory.* New Haven, Conn.

WALKER, C. E., GUEST, R. H. and TURNER, A. N. 1956: *The foreman on the assembly line.* Cambridge, Mass.

WARNER, W. L. and LOW, J. O. 1947: *The social system of the modern factory.* New Haven, Conn.

WEINSTOCK, S. A. 1963: 'Role elements: a link between acculturation and occupational status', *BJS* **14**.

WHYTE, W. F. 1952: 'Economic incentives and human relations', *Harv. Bus. Rev.* **30**.

WHYTE, W. F. and DALTON, M. 1958: *Money and motivation.* New York.

WHYTE, W. H. 1960: *The organization man.* London.

WILENSKY, H. 1961: 'Orderly career patterns and social participation: the impact of work history on social integration in the middle class', *ASR* **26**, 521–39.

YOUNG, M. 1958: *The rise of the meritocracy.* London.

Index

ability, 31 32, 34, 43, 56, 57, 59, 107, 108, 122, 134, 139
achievement principle, 2, 27; as basis of society, 40–46; and social status, 47–53; and occupational role identity, 54–78; and promotion, 78–99; and wages, 100–133; historically assessed, 134–43
achieving society, 8, 11, 14, 15, 17, 18, 32, 33, 34, 40–46, 126, 134
age, 43
agriculture, 23
Althusser, L., 8
automation, 19–20, 121, 135

Bahrdt, H., 72, 80, 81, 84, 106, 136
Bakke, E., 76
Baldamus, W., 71, 109, 112, 115, 116, 117, 124, 136–7
Baran, P. A., 20
Barber, B., 49
Bates, H., 107
Beale, L. V., 63
Becker, H., 61, 62, 79, 91, 93
Behrend, H., 112, 125, 127, 130
Bendix, R., 54, 66, 78, 147
Bensman, J., 58–9, 83
Berger, P., 57, 58, 136
Blau, P. M., 62, 79
Brayfield, A. H., 122
bureaucratic ritualism, 61, 73

capital owners, 14
Caplow, T., 47, 88
Carper, J., 61, 62
central role elements, 54, 60, 73, 76, 82
Chinoy, E., 78
Claessens, P., 69
class, 7–8, 66, 67, 130–31
Coates, C. H., 64
Colins, O., 89, 90, 130–32
critical theory, 4
Crockett, H., 58

Crockett, W. H., 122

Dahrendorf, R., 11, 24, 59
Dalton, M., 70, 93, 94, 130–32
Davies, A. F., 51
Davis, K., 48–50, 110
decision-making, 15, 17, 21, 29
Dichgans, H., 83
discrimination, 2, 32, 43, 134; ethnic, 43, 85, 92–7; religious, 85, 95; sexual, 43, 85–6
disqualification, 24
division of labour, 23, 24, 75, 78, 96
Dornbusch, S. M., 114
Dreitzel, H. P., 60, 134
Dreyfuss, C., 80, 97
Drucker, P. F., 142

economic growth, 16
education, 20, 23, 32, 39, 82, 83, 88, 94, 108–11
'efficiency', 12, 112
elite groups, 11
employment level, 18
employment structure, 18, 86, 109
Engels, F., 8
entrepreneurs, 11
ethnomethodology, 6
Etzioni, A., 53
Euler, H., 108, 124
Evans, J. W., 63
extrafunctional orientations, 30, 56, 66 (see also peripheral role elements); acquired in training, 61–4; social distribution of, 66–70; and job satisfaction, 71–2; and self identity, 73–8; and occupational mobility 78–99, 116

family, 18, 32, 86, 110, 138–40
Faunce, W. A., 120, 121
Foa, U. G., 88
Foote, N. N., 77
forces of production, 5

Form, W. H., 87
Friedmann, E. A., 76
Friedrichs, G., 121
Froomkin, J., 51
Fuhrmann, J., 69
full employment, 16, 19
functional differentiation, 24, 26, 27, 39
functional importance, 48–53, 105, 112
functionalism, 4, 6
functionalist stratification theory, 50, 105–7, 138–9

Galbraith, J. K., 15
Gehlen, A., 72, 74
Gembardt, U., 82
German Industrialists' Association, 12.
Gitelman, H. M., 79
Glick, P., 109
Goodman, P. S., 113
Gouldner, A. W., 106
Greenwood, E., 76

Habermas, J., 7, 20
Hack, L., 135
Hartfiel, G., 69
Hartmann, H., 106, 107
Havinghurst, R. J., 76
Heilbronner, R., 16
Heitbaum, H., 113, 118, 120
Hertzler, J. O., 78, 80
Hetzler, H. W., 118, 119, 121, 125, 132
hierarchical differentiation, 24, 26, 27, 39
Hoffmann, R., 101, 102
Hofmann, W., 101
Hyman, H., 58

Icheiser, G., 60
ideology, 12, 13–14, 16, 21, 83, 124, 134
individual discretion, 30
individualistic income orientation, 129–31, 133
industrial militancy, 1
initiatory influence, 33, 36, 54, 127, 129
institutional loyalty, 28, 66, 68, 90
Institut für Sozialforschung, 71
Institut für Wirtschaftsforschung, 113, 124
interest groups, 5, 14
internal controls, 29, 140
investment, 17

Jacques, E., 113–14, 119
Jaffe, A. J., 51
job evaluation, 3, 119–23
job satisfaction, 71–6, 116
Jüres, A., 81

Kesting, J., 81
Keynesian economics, 9, 19
Kluth, H., 40–41
knowledge, 28, 31, 49, 59, 77, 79, 94, 108, 139
Kornhauser, A., 115
Kosiol, E., 103, 118
Krelle, W., 101
Kriesberg, L., 51, 52, 63, 124

labour market, 18, 19, 86, 109
labour turnover, 129
legal system, 33
legitimation, 1, 6, 21, 32, 41
leisure, 75
Lenski, G., 47, 49
Lipset, S. M., 65, 66, 78
Livernash, E., 115, 116
Lockwood, D., 7, 69
Lovenstein, M., 16
Luckmann, T., 57, 58, 136
Lutz, B. 36, 37, 102, 121, 122, 128

Malm, F. T., 65
manual workers, 68–70, 73
marginal groups, 20
marginal productivity, 43, 44, 100–102
Marsh, R. M., 59
Marshall, T. H., 142
Marx, K., 5, 7, 8, 98, 99
marxism, 4, 6, 111
Mechanic, D., 106
Merton, R. K., 55, 61, 63, 64
middle class, 73, 86, 130
military organizations, 27
Miller, D. C., 87, 149
Miller, H. P., 109
Mills, C. W., 6, 69, 83, 90
Mills, D. L., 77
monopolization, 14
Moore, W. E., 48–50, 110
Morse, N. C., 75, 76
Mouzelis, N., 7
Muntz, E. E., 108, 109

Negt, O., 11
normative control, 35, 36
normative orientations, 9, 28–32, 38, 54, 64, 67, 80, 111–12
norms, 32, 33, 34

Nosow, S., 96, 97

Obert, H., 109
occupational ideology, 56, 62
occupational mobility, 47, 68–70, 100
(*see also* promotion); blockages, 80;
chances of, 69; orientation to, 58,
60–78; strategies of, 70, 73
occupational prestige, 48–53
occupational recruitment, 3, 42, 78,
85, 87
occupational role identity, 54–60; and
social mobility, 60–78
occupational socialization, 63, 68
occupational symbols, 56
Offe, C., 7, 8, 21
organizational change, 54, 106, 125,
137
organized capitalism, 15
Ott, J., 67

Parsons, T., 98
peer groups, 32
Pellegrin, H. J., 64, 107
performance, 54, 56, 121, 134, 136,
137
peripheral role elements, 66–78 (*see
also* extrafunctional orientations)
physical strength, 23, 111
piece-rates, 122–3
political parties, 14
Pollock, F., 23
Popitz, H., 66, 81
poverty, 20
power, 34, 105, 131
Preiser, E., 101
preventive influence, 36, 37, 39
productivity, 44, 105–7, 115, 125, 132,
134
professionalization, 70, 76
professions, 77, 141
promotion, 3, 54, 59, 69, 70, 88;
criteria for, 81–4 (*see also* occupational mobility)
public opinion, 11

qualifications, 23, 24, 26, 36, 62, 83,
90, 108–11

raw material industries, 23
Reder, W., 108
reference groups, 63
regulatory norms, 30, 34, 60, 121
127, 140, 143
relations of production, 5
Reichwein, R., 103, 152
relative deprivation, 34

religion, 75 (*see also* discrimination,
religious)
responsibility, 49, 50, 107–14, 119
retraining, 79
Reynolds, L., 79
Ridgeway, V. F., 123
Rogoff, N., 79
Roper, E., 93–4, 97
Rosen, B. C., 58, 66
Rosenberg, B., 58–9
Rowntree, J. and M., 20
Roy, D., 130–33

Saint-Simon, H. de, 41
Schaefer, W., 113
Schein, E. H., 67
Schneider, L., 114
Schumpeter, J. A., 101
Seeman, M., 63
seniority, 84
sexuality, 75
Sheppard, H. J., 12
Shimmin, S., 123
Simmons, O. G., 76
Simon, H. A., 27
Simpson, R. L. and I. H., 49, 50
skills, 3, 30, 59, 93
Slocum, W. L., 47, 66, 75, 84–6, 88
Smigel, E. O., 91–3
social conflict, 8, 34, 131
social inequality, 41
social mobility, 42, 47, 57 (*see also*
occupational mobility)
social welfare policy, 18, 102–3, 116
socialization, primary, 21, 34, 64, 69,
112, 117; secondary, 21, 34, 112,
116
socialization agencies, 32
specialization, 23, 24, 39, 77, 78, 119
Stammer, O., 69
state, 14, 16
status, 47, 56, 78, 80, 128, 141
status allocation, 54, 73, 86, 139, 142
status consciousness, 58, 63
status groups, 21, 33
Stevens, H., 118, 125
Stinchcombe, A. L., 36
Stone, B., 66, 68–70
Strauss, A. L., 79, 91, 93
Sweezy, P. M., 20
symbolic interactionism, 6

task-continuous organizations, 2, 25,
26, 36, 39
task-discontinuous organizations, 2,
25, 26, 30, 31, 39, 78, 79, 82, 106

technical rules, 1, 28, 29, 32, 34, 111–112, 114
technological change, 3, 19, 54–5, 106, 112, 113, 116, 125, 128, 133, 137
Theobald, R., 18
time-and-motion study, 3, 118
training, 18, 20, 23, 24, 28, 43, 61, 107–11
Tumin, M. M., 48, 110, 138–41

'unemployables', 19
unemployment, 76, 135–6

Vidich, A., 83
Vollmer, H. M., 77
voluntary associations, 14
Vroom, V. H., 71, 75

wage differentials, 1, 3, 42, 43; conventional explanations of, 100–105; and labour productivity, 105–7; and education, 108–11; and effort, 111–13; and responsibility, 114; based on norms, 114–17; and work study, 118–26; as incentives, 126–33
wage levels, 3
Warner, W. L., 85
Weinstock, S. A., 60
Weiss, R. S., 75
white collar workers, 68, 69, 73
Whyte, W. F., 131
Whyte, W. H., 67, 87
Wilensky, H. L., 75
Willener, A., 36, 37, 121, 122
work ethic, 31, 60
work role, 27, 31, 59, 108 (*see also* occupational role identity)
work stress, 107–14, 119
work study, 118–26
working conditions, 54, 72, 75, 111, 119

Young, M., 135

Zirwas, H., 69